A GRATITUDE JOURNAL
FOR KIDS BY

UNLOCKING YOUR
POTENTIAL TO THRIVE

THEAWESOMEINC.CO.NZ

FOCUS
on the GOOD
SOON
you will
SEE MORE
ENJOY MORE
APPRECIATE
MORE

IT IS THE SIMPLE THINGS IN LIFE THAT CAN REALLY MAKE YOU FEEL HAPPY, IF YOU STOP AND NOTICE.

Sometimes life can get you down, so this book is all about helping you think of the things that are truly great about being alive.

Practising gratitude each day makes you feel good, makes you smarter, healthier and over time can really help on those days that aren't so great (we all have those from time to time). Go to the back of the book to find some more awesome facts about how practising gratitude helps you.

Look at our example (page 7), you can see a GRATITUDE section where each day you fill in at least three new things that you are grateful for. There are literally hundreds of things that we can be thankful for like hanging out with your friends, doctors to help if we are sick, a roof over our heads, our family, our body and all of the amazing things it can do, food to eat, a sunny day, feeling loved by someone .... so many things if you stop and notice. Use our prompts on page 6 if you get stuck.

You will also see a HAPPINESS SCALE on the edge of each page. Colour this in and it will give you a great idea of how happy you have been when you flick back through the pages. If you aren't so happy most of the time, maybe you need to talk to someone about what could be making you feel so low. So, each day make sure to colour in your happiness scale based on how you feel that day.

We have also included a BLANK FACE for you to fill in what mood you are in today. Are you happy, content or excited? Or are you feeling sad, angry or anxious? Don't be afraid to express your feelings, sometimes it can help you to understand them.

Scattered throughout the pages of this book you will find some fun activities too... Fill in a little about yourself, what makes you happy, things you love, and awesome things that happen to you. Sometimes it will be the little things that were great like a hug someone gave you when you felt upset, or playing computer games. Get creative and use lots of colour.

There are also pages with SELF-CARE and HAPPINESS TIPS and COLOURING IN pages drawn by kids like you! Did you know that concentrating on something like colouring can help if you are feeling anxious or stressed. So, if you are feeling overwhelmed or angry, sad or bored, open up this journal and create a masterpiece.

This journal is all about changing the way we look at things AND the way we think about things. The world we live in can be a little crazy at times, there is a lot of pressure to have the right clothing, computer games and other stuff. There is pressure to look a certain way and to be the best at something. It can all get overwhelming, but with gratitude as part of your life you will soon realise that all that stuff isn't what makes you happy. Happiness can't be bought at a store, it is the simple things in life, like playing on the beach and laughing with friends.

NOTHING COMPLICATED, JUST SIMPLE STUFF.

We challenge you to try and complete this book and we would love for you to tell us (or your parents) how it makes you feel at the end when you can read back all that positive stuff you have written about.

Remember AWESOME ENDS IN ME – you are unique, irreplaceable and awesome!

We hope you love this journal.
With the hugest gratitude,

AWESOME INC

IF YOU GET STUCK USE THESE EXAMPLES FOR INSPIRATION

TODAY I AM GRATEFUL FOR...

1. The sun is shining and it makes me feel HAPPY!

2. I scored a goal and my team won

3. My legs because they help me run fast

THANK YOU, THANK YOU, THANK YOU
FOR ALL THE AMAZING THINGS IN MY LIFE!

25 WAYS TO >> YOU <<

LOOK AFTER

SIT IN
NATURE

TURN OFF
ALL ELECTRONICS

DANCE LIKE
NO-ONE IS WATCHING

TAKE A
SHOWER OR BATH

MAKE
YOUR BED

WALK BAREFOOT
ON THE GRASS

HAVE A
HEALTHY SNACK

TALK TO
A FRIEND

HUG
A PET

WRITE IN
THIS JOURN

DO
SOMETHING
NEW

READ
A BOOK

GO FOR
A RUN

CLIME
A TREE

SIT IN
THE SUN

DO SOME
COLOURING IN

LAY ON YOUR BACK
AND WATCH THE CLOUDS

GO FOR
A WALK

LISTEN
TO MUSIC

TAKE SOME
DEEP BELLY BREATHS

VISUALISE
SOMETHING
AWESOME

CHANGE
YOUR
ENVIRONMENT

DO SOME
MEDITATION

WATCH
SOMETHING
FUNNY

DO SOMETHING
NICE FOR SOMEO

WHEN YOU ARE FEELING DOWN, USE THESE IDEAS FOR SOME SELF-CARE.

ALL ABOUT
ME

THIS PERSON
IS AMAZINGLY
AWESOME!

AGE

FAVOURITE COLOUR

BOOKS I LOVE ...

NAME

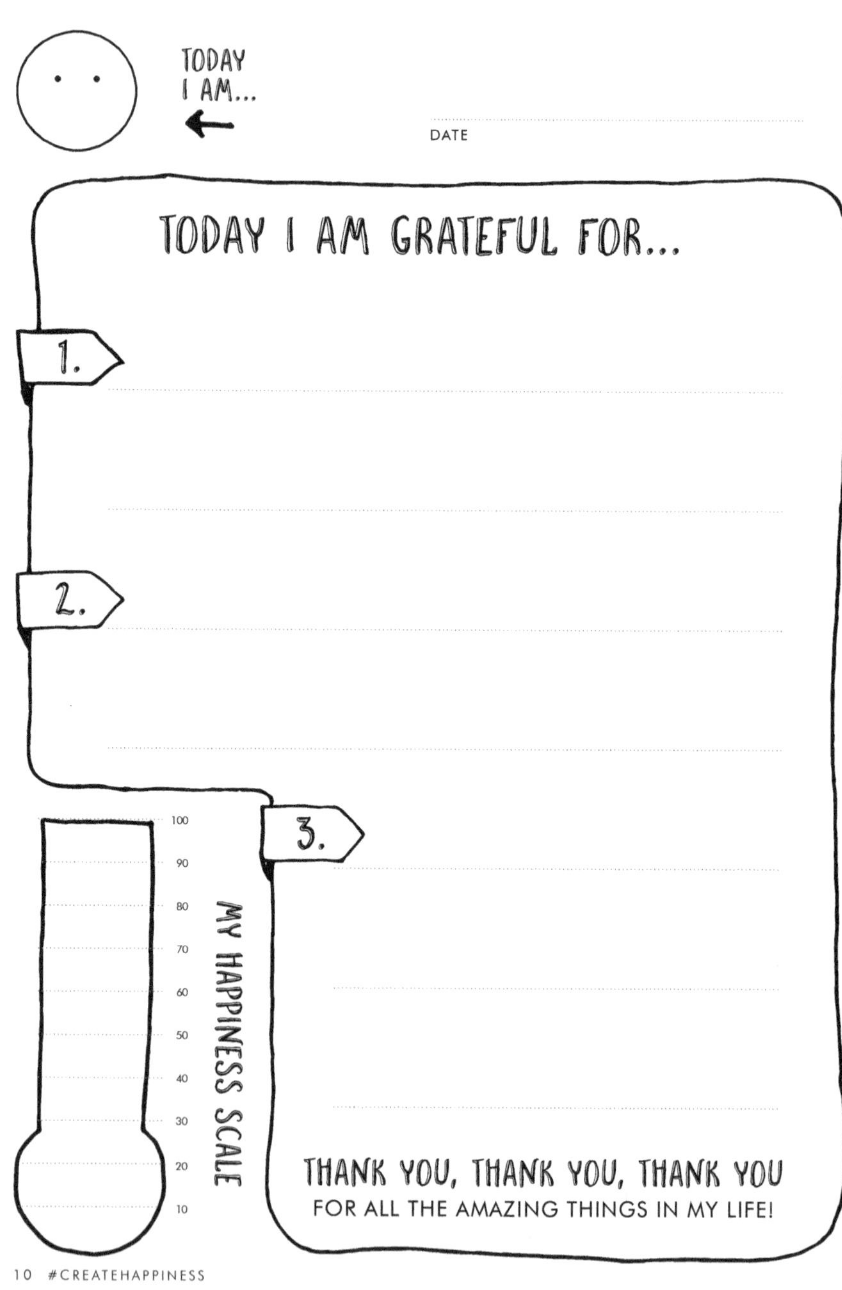

TODAY
I AM...
TODAY I AM GRATEFUL FOR...
DATE
1.
2.
3.
100
90
80
70
60
50
40
30
20
10
MY HAPPINESS SCALE
THANK YOU, THANK YOU, THANK YOU
FOR ALL THE AMAZING THINGS IN MY LIFE!

DATE

TODAY I AM GRATEFUL FOR...

1.

2.

3.

THANK YOU, THANK YOU, THANK YOU
FOR ALL THE AMAZING THINGS IN MY LIFE!

MY HAPPINESS SCALE

100
90
80
70
60
50
40
30
20
10

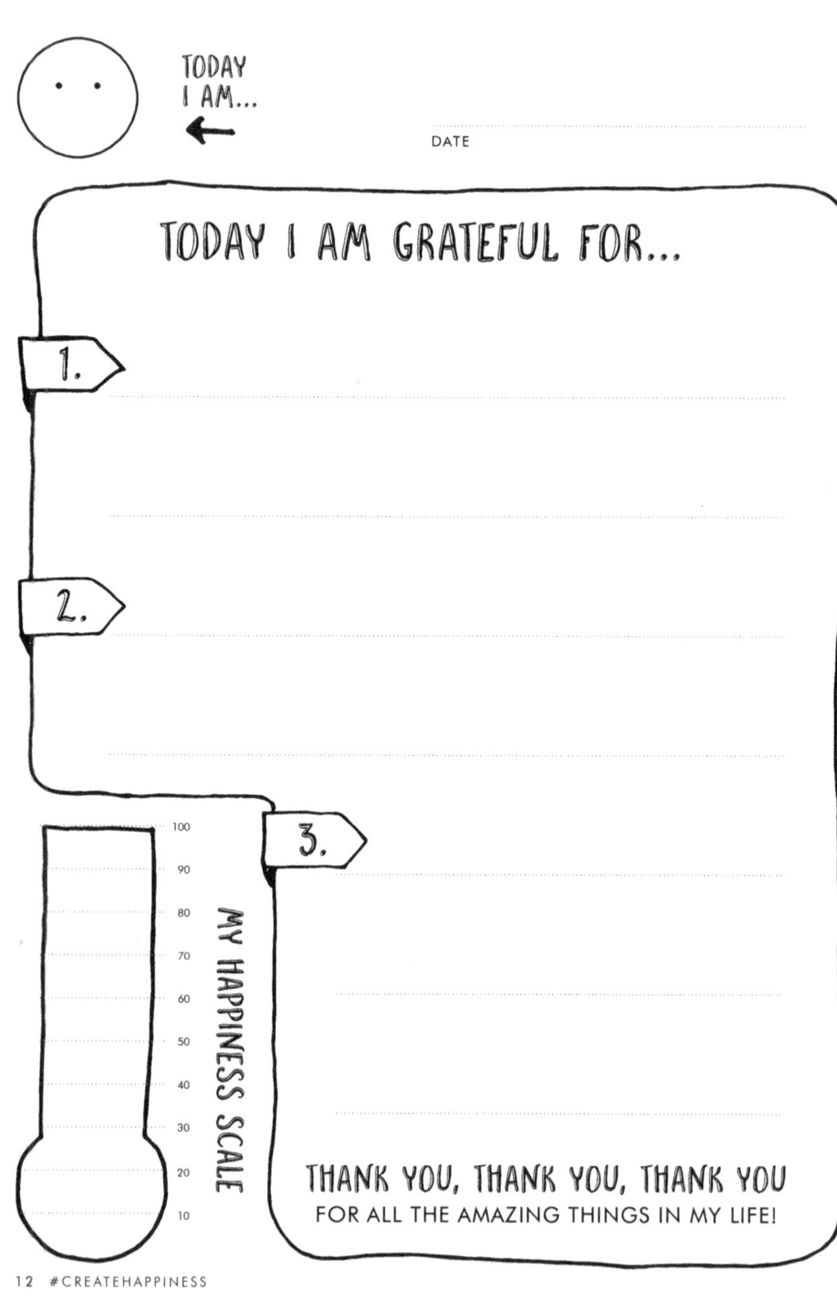
TODAY
I AM...

DATE

TODAY I AM GRATEFUL FOR...

1.

2.

3.

100
90
80
70
60
50
40
30
20
10

MY HAPPINESS SCALE

THANK YOU, THANK YOU, THANK YOU
FOR ALL THE AMAZING THINGS IN MY LIFE!

DATE

TODAY I AM GRATEFUL FOR...

1.

2.

3.

THANK YOU, THANK YOU, THANK YOU
FOR ALL THE AMAZING THINGS IN MY LIFE!

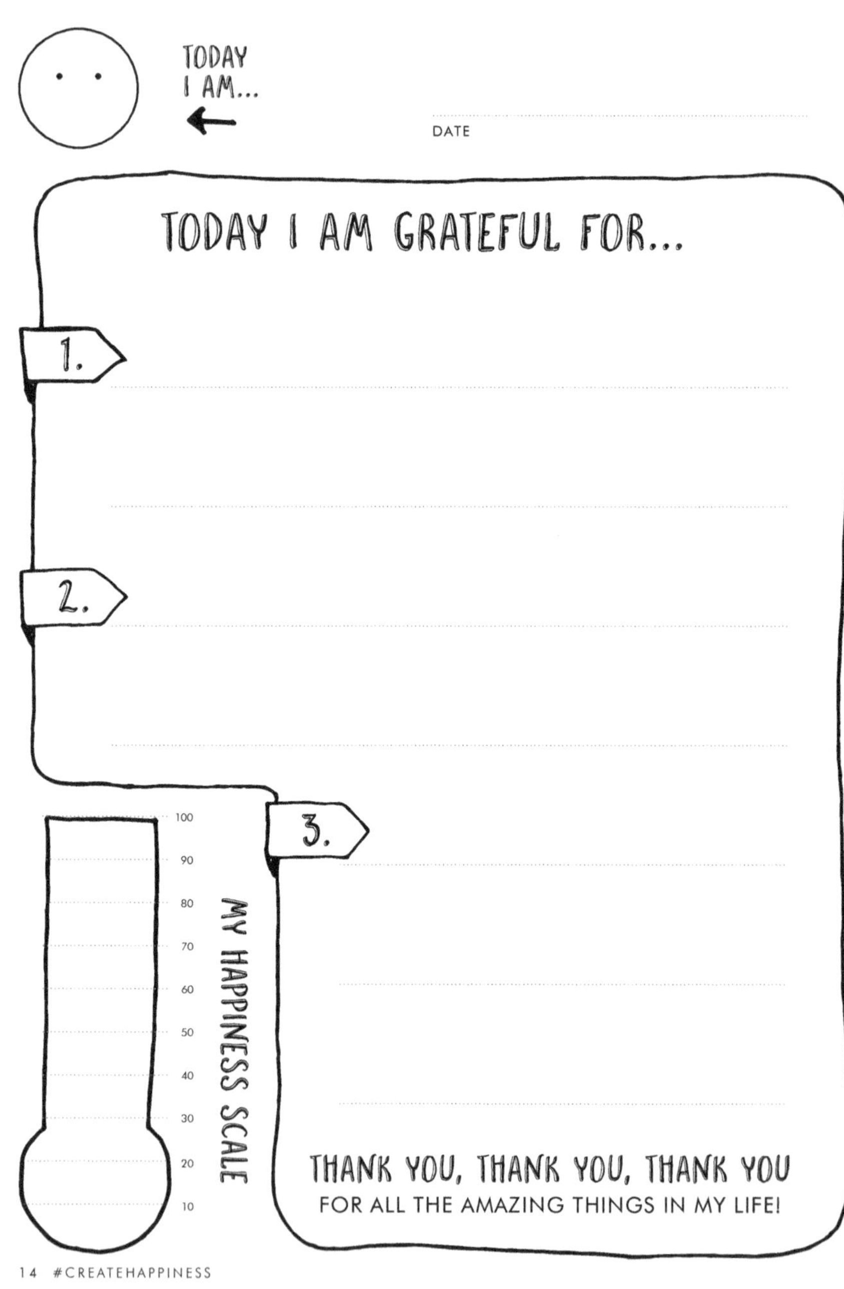

TODAY
I AM...
DATE
TODAY I AM GRATEFUL FOR...
1.
2.
3.
100
90
80
70
60
50
40
30
20
10
MY HAPPINESS SCALE
THANK YOU, THANK YOU, THANK YOU
FOR ALL THE AMAZING THINGS IN MY LIFE!

DATE

TODAY I AM GRATEFUL FOR...

1.

2.

3.

THANK YOU, THANK YOU, THANK YOU
FOR ALL THE AMAZING THINGS IN MY LIFE!

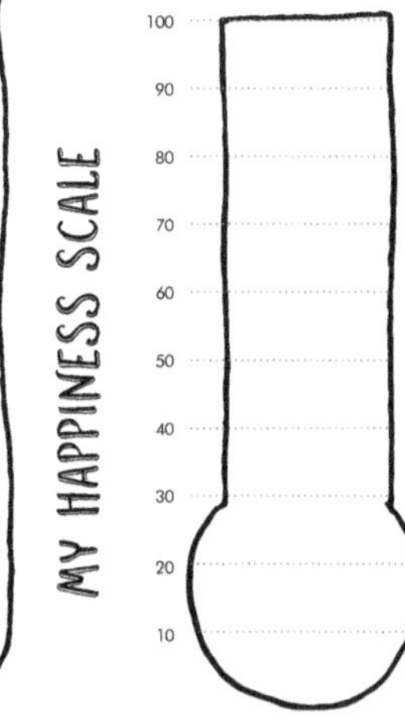

TODAY I AM...
DATE
TODAY I AM GRATEFUL FOR...
1.
2.
3.
100
90
80
70
60
50
40
30
20
10
MY HAPPINESS SCALE
THANK YOU, THANK YOU, THANK YOU
FOR ALL THE AMAZING THINGS IN MY LIFE!

DATE

TODAY I AM GRATEFUL FOR...

1.

2.

3.

THANK YOU, THANK YOU, THANK YOU
FOR ALL THE AMAZING THINGS IN MY LIFE!

MY HAPPINESS SCALE

100
90
80
70
60
50
40
30
20
10

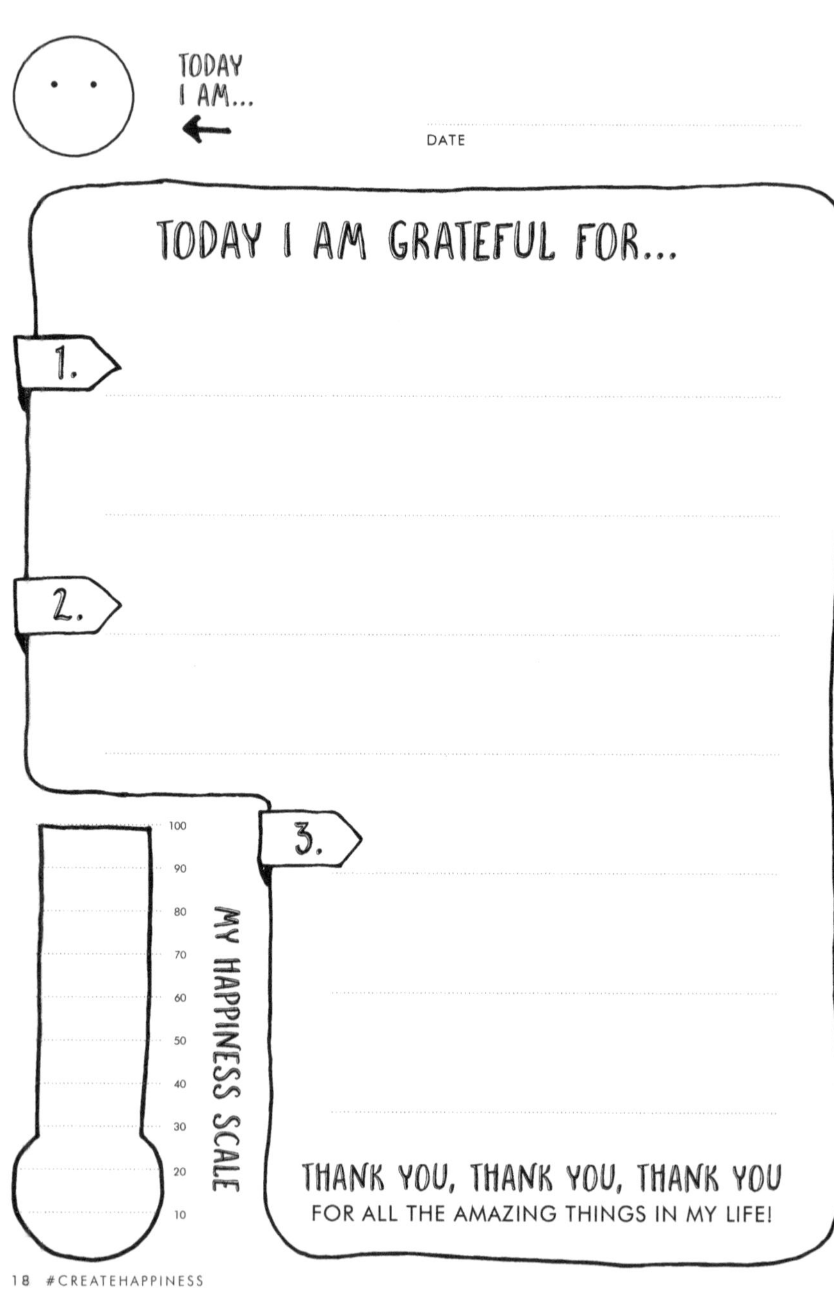

TODAY
I AM...
TODAY I AM GRATEFUL FOR...
DATE
1.
2.
3.
MY HAPPINESS SCALE
100
90
80
70
60
50
40
30
20
10
THANK YOU, THANK YOU, THANK YOU
FOR ALL THE AMAZING THINGS IN MY LIFE!

TODAY I AM...

TODAY I AM GRATEFUL FOR...

1.

2.

3.

THANK YOU, THANK YOU, THANK YOU
FOR ALL THE AMAZING THINGS IN MY LIFE!

MY HAPPINESS SCALE

100
90
80
70
60
50
40
30
20
10

LAUGHTER is the BEST MEDICINE

HAPPINESS TIP:

Laugh as much as you can, whenever you can, and learn to laugh at yourself too ... it is the best medicine. Even if you force yourself to laugh, by faking it, for long enough, at some point you will genuinely start laughing.

Laughter can strengthen your immune system, help boost your energy and diminish pain, and also protect you from the effects of stress.

WHAT MAKES ME LAUGH...

USE WORDS AND PICTURES TO DESCRIBE WHAT MAKES YOU LAUGH

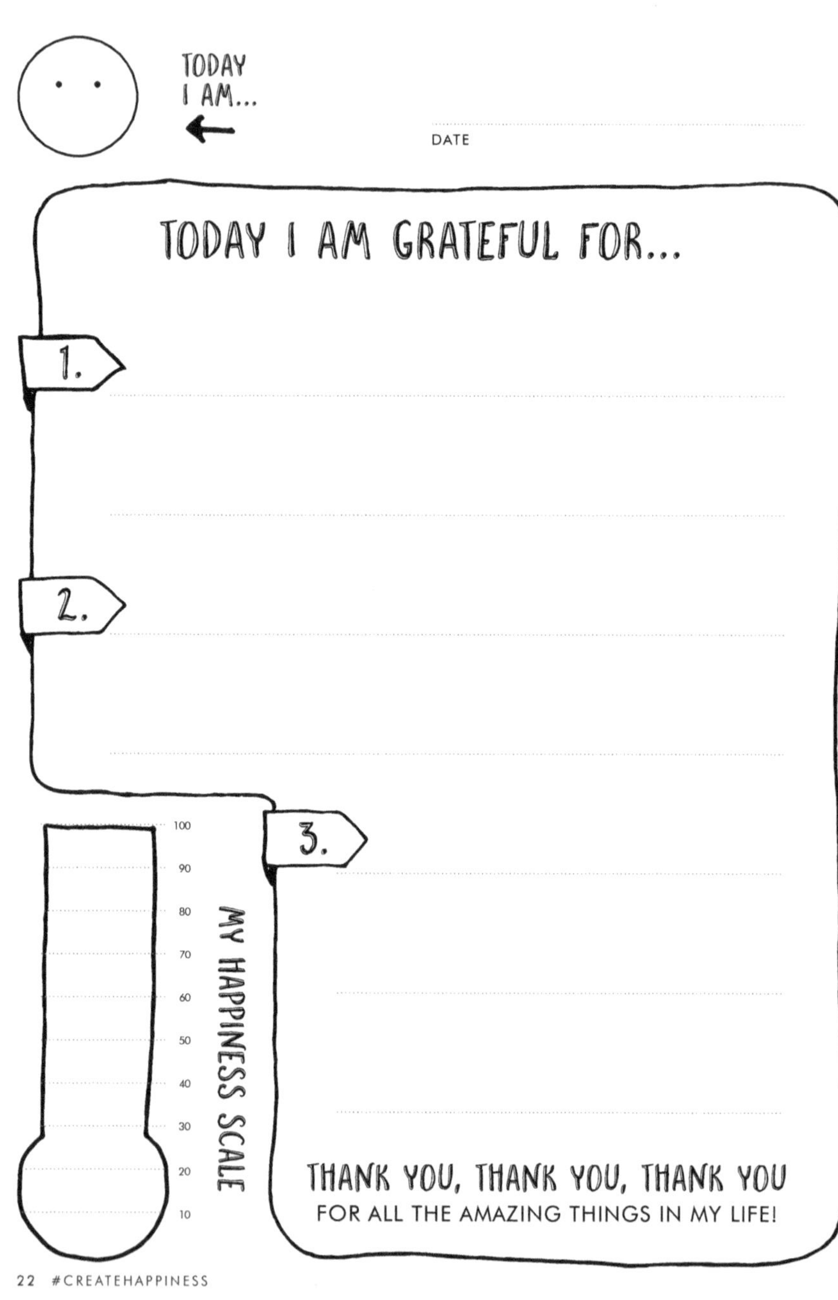
TODAY
I AM...

DATE

TODAY I AM GRATEFUL FOR...

1.

2.

3.

100
90
80
70
60
50
40
30
20
10

MY HAPPINESS SCALE

THANK YOU, THANK YOU, THANK YOU
FOR ALL THE AMAZING THINGS IN MY LIFE!

TODAY
I AM...
→

TODAY I AM GRATEFUL FOR...

1.

2.

3.

THANK YOU, THANK YOU, THANK YOU
FOR ALL THE AMAZING THINGS IN MY LIFE!

MY HAPPINESS SCALE

100
90
80
70
60
50
40
30
20
10

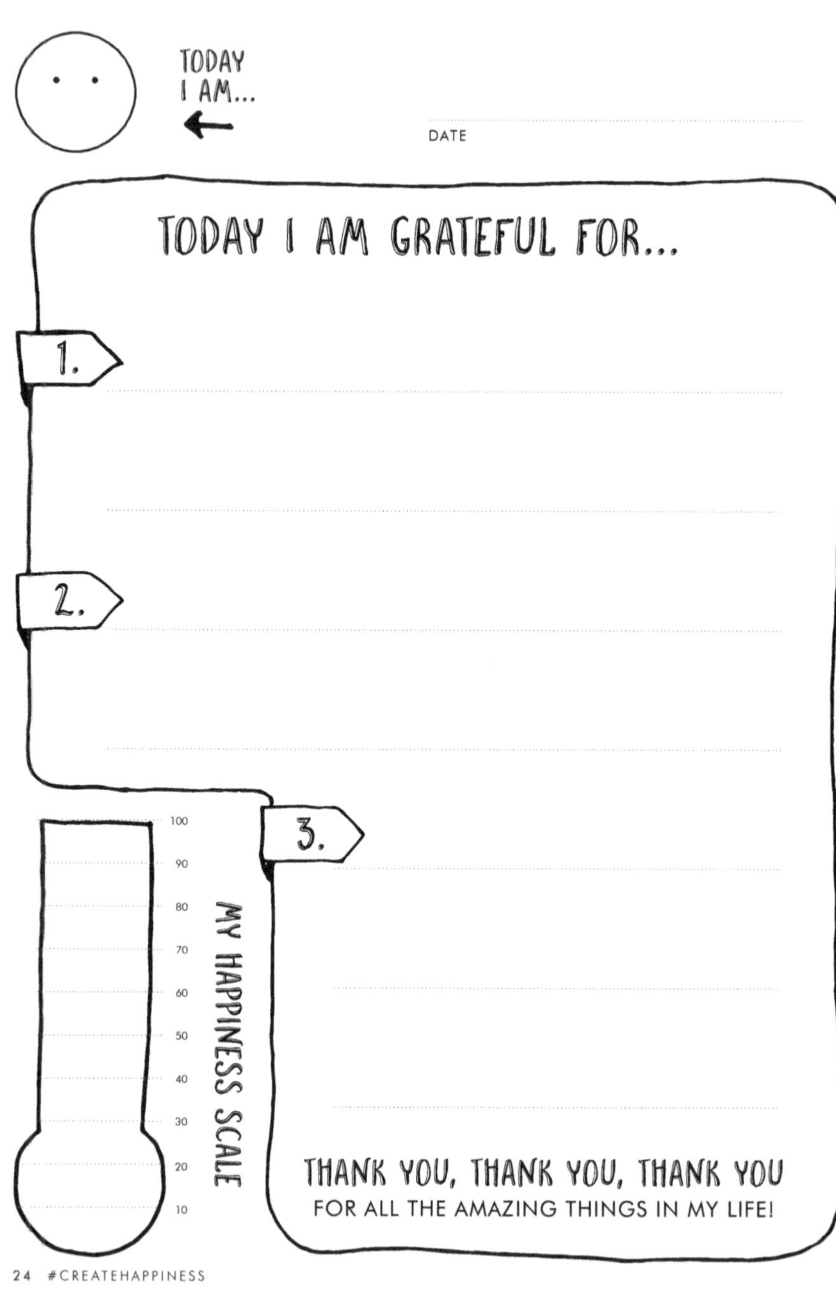

TODAY
I AM...
DATE
TODAY I AM GRATEFUL FOR...
1.
2.
3.
100
90
80
70
60
50
40
30
20
10
MY HAPPINESS SCALE
THANK YOU, THANK YOU, THANK YOU
FOR ALL THE AMAZING THINGS IN MY LIFE!

____
DATE

TODAY I AM GRATEFUL FOR...

1.

2.

3.

THANK YOU, THANK YOU, THANK YOU
FOR ALL THE AMAZING THINGS IN MY LIFE!

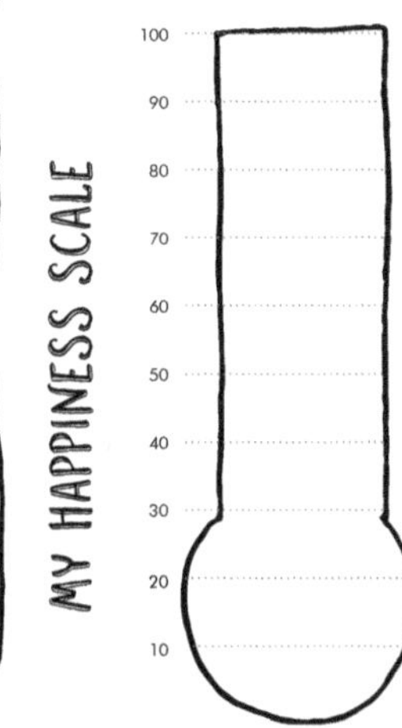

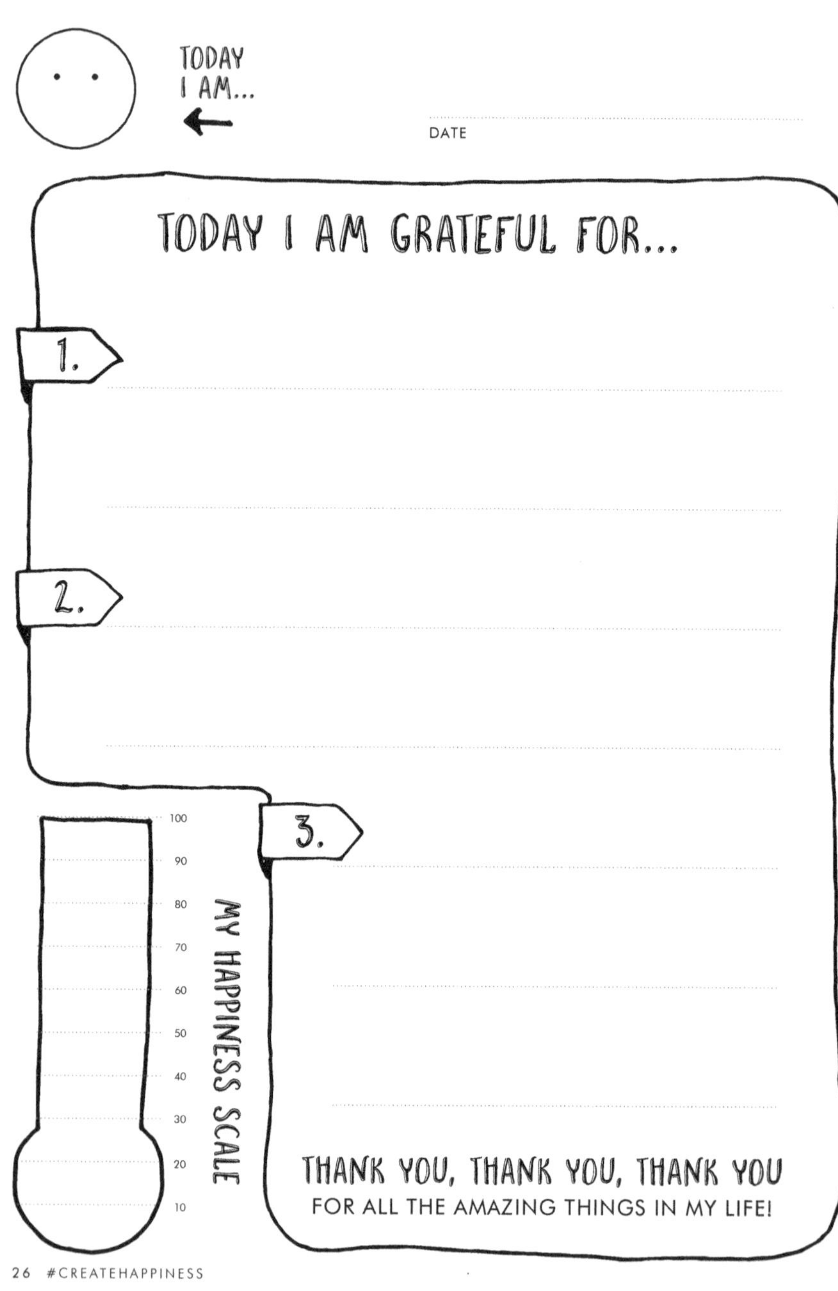

TODAY
I AM...
DATE
TODAY I AM GRATEFUL FOR...
1.
2.
3.
100
90
80
70
60
50
40
30
20
10
MY HAPPINESS SCALE
THANK YOU, THANK YOU, THANK YOU
FOR ALL THE AMAZING THINGS IN MY LIFE!

DATE

TODAY I AM GRATEFUL FOR...

1.

2.

3.

THANK YOU, THANK YOU, THANK YOU
FOR ALL THE AMAZING THINGS IN MY LIFE!

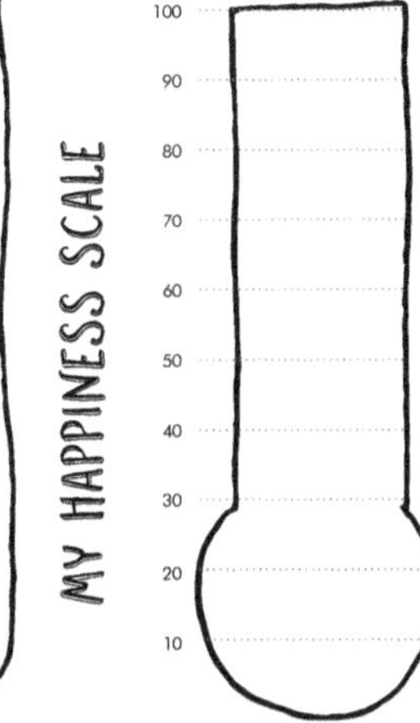

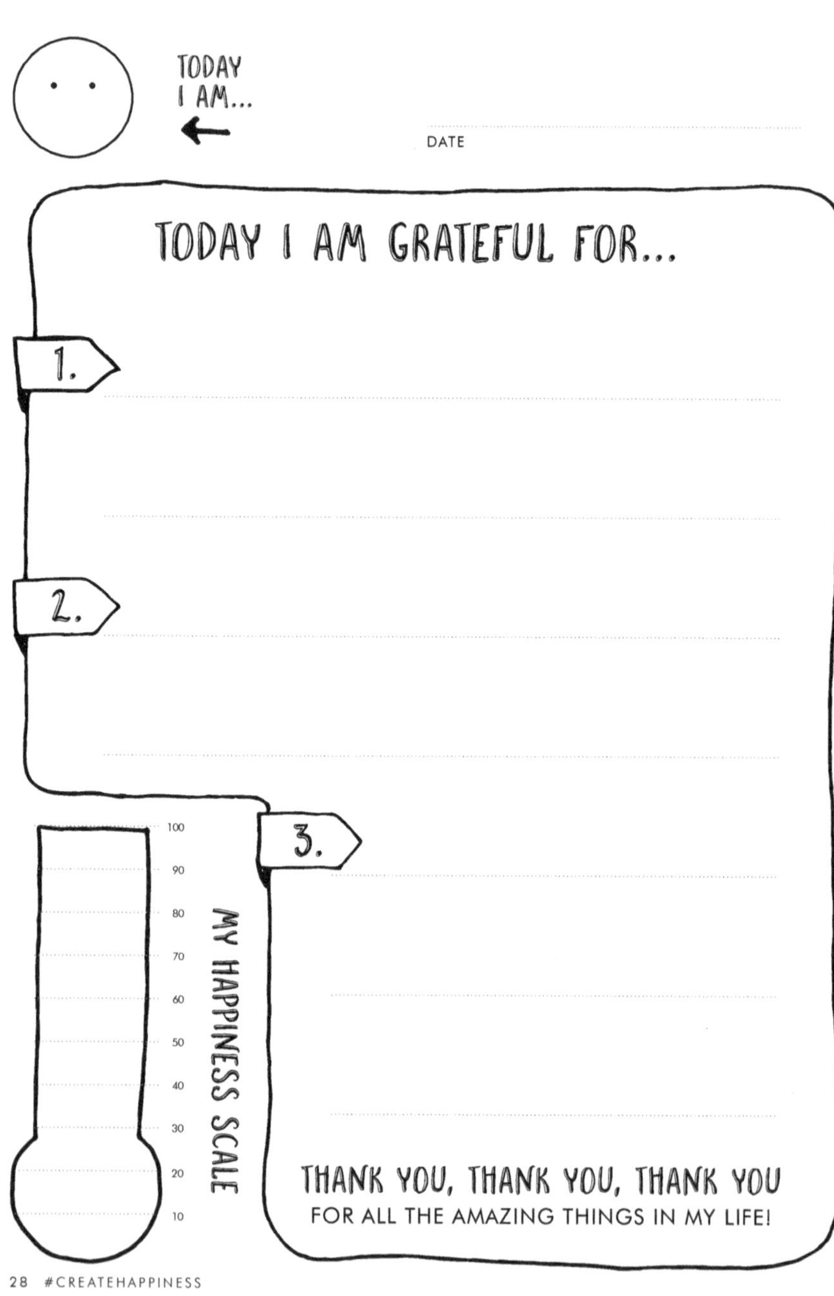

TODAY I AM...
DATE
TODAY I AM GRATEFUL FOR...
1.
2.
3.
100
90
80
70
60
50
40
30
20
10
MY HAPPINESS SCALE
THANK YOU, THANK YOU, THANK YOU
FOR ALL THE AMAZING THINGS IN MY LIFE!

DATE

TODAY I AM GRATEFUL FOR...

1.

2.

3.

THANK YOU, THANK YOU, THANK YOU
FOR ALL THE AMAZING THINGS IN MY LIFE!

MY HAPPINESS SCALE

100
90
80
70
60
50
40
30
20
10

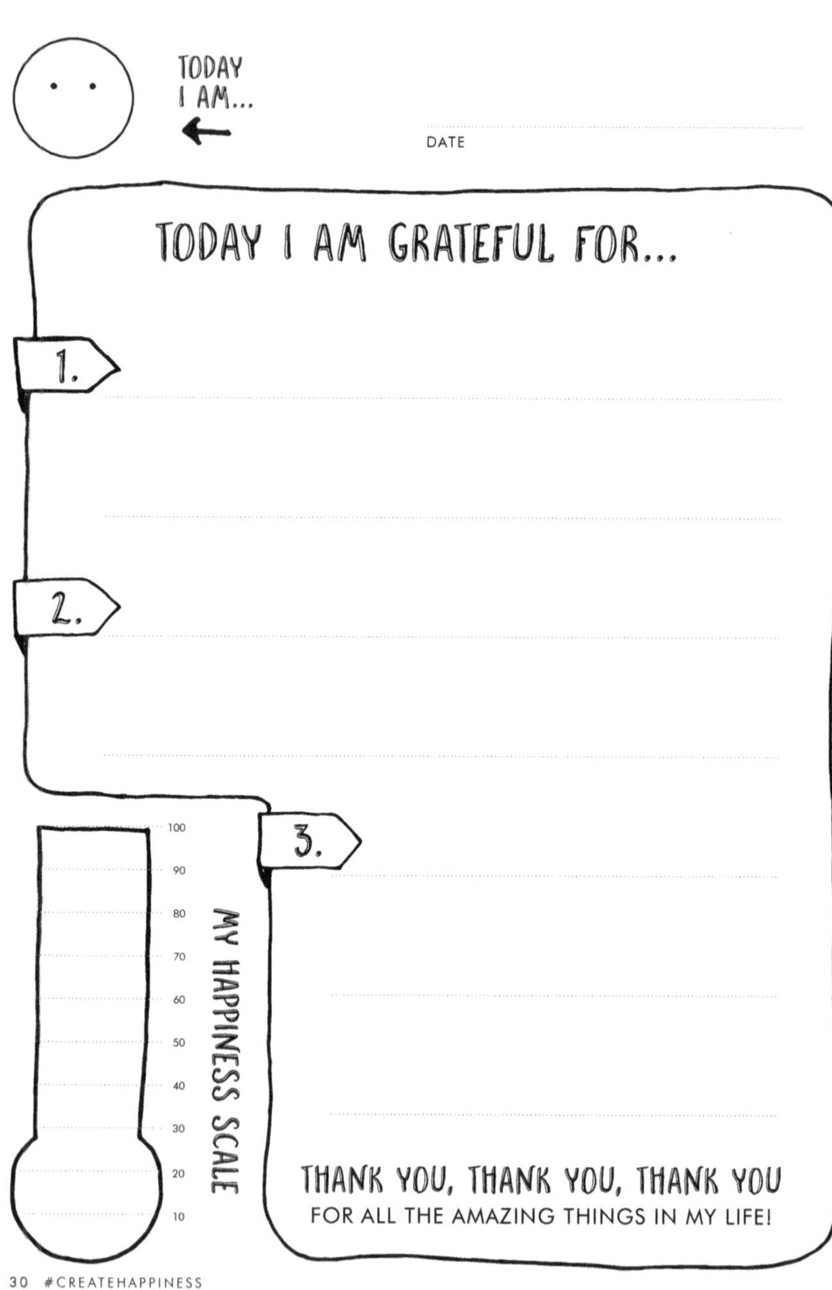

TODAY
I AM...
DATE
TODAY I AM GRATEFUL FOR...
1.
2.
3.
100
90
80
70
60
50
40
30
20
10
MY HAPPINESS SCALE
THANK YOU, THANK YOU, THANK YOU
FOR ALL THE AMAZING THINGS IN MY LIFE!

DRAWING BY LEO, AGE 9

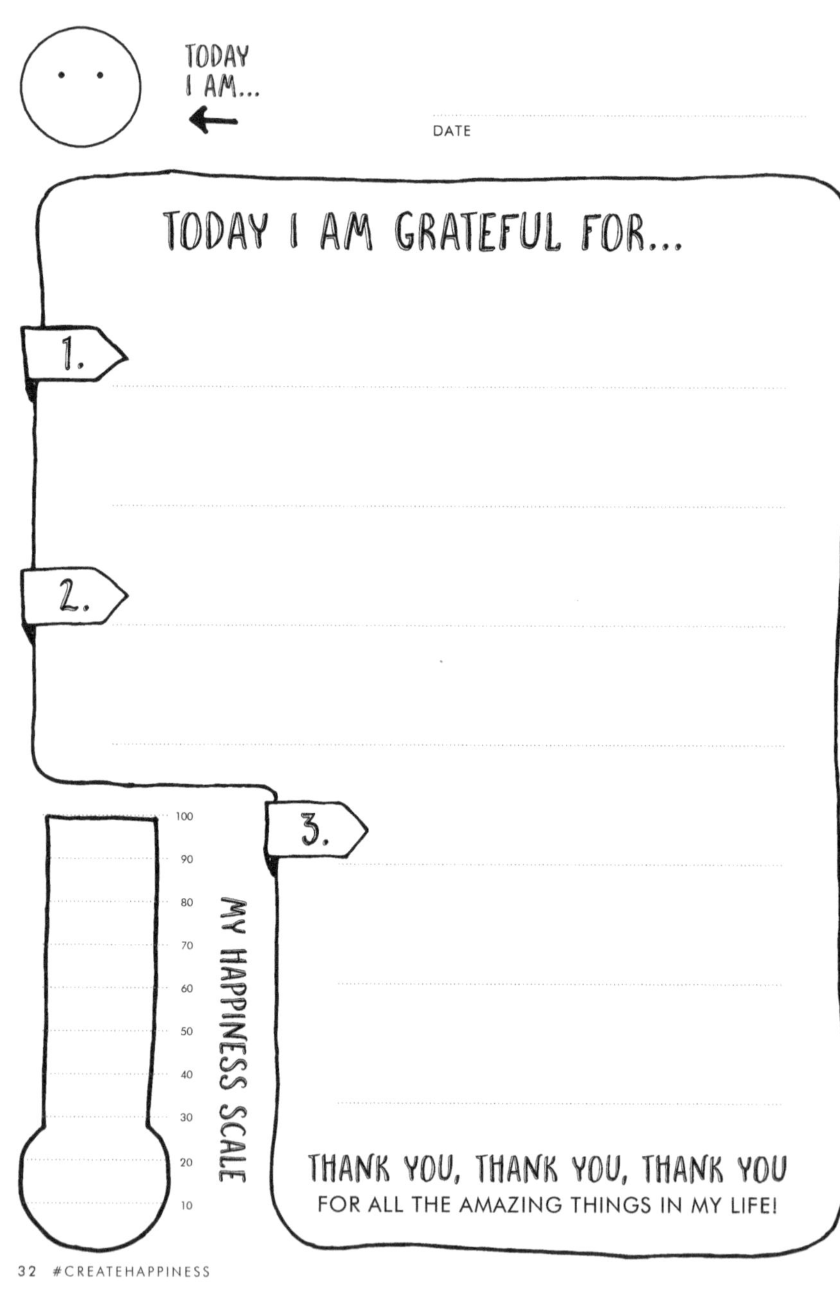

TODAY I AM...
DATE
TODAY I AM GRATEFUL FOR...
1.
2.
3.
100
90
80
70
60
50
40
30
20
10
MY HAPPINESS SCALE
THANK YOU, THANK YOU, THANK YOU
FOR ALL THE AMAZING THINGS IN MY LIFE!

TODAY I AM... →

TODAY I AM GRATEFUL FOR...

1.

2.

3.

THANK YOU, THANK YOU, THANK YOU
FOR ALL THE AMAZING THINGS IN MY LIFE!

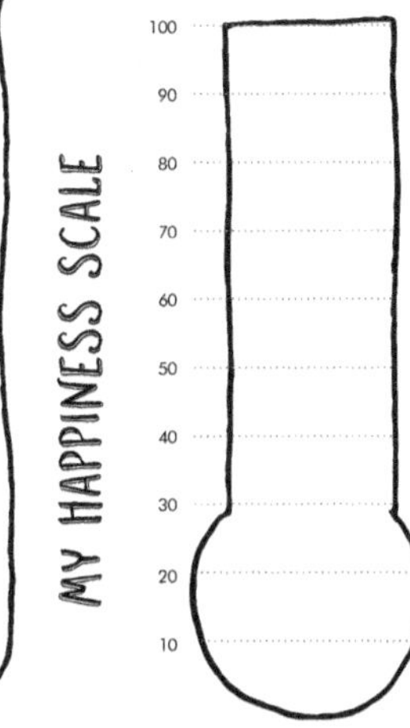

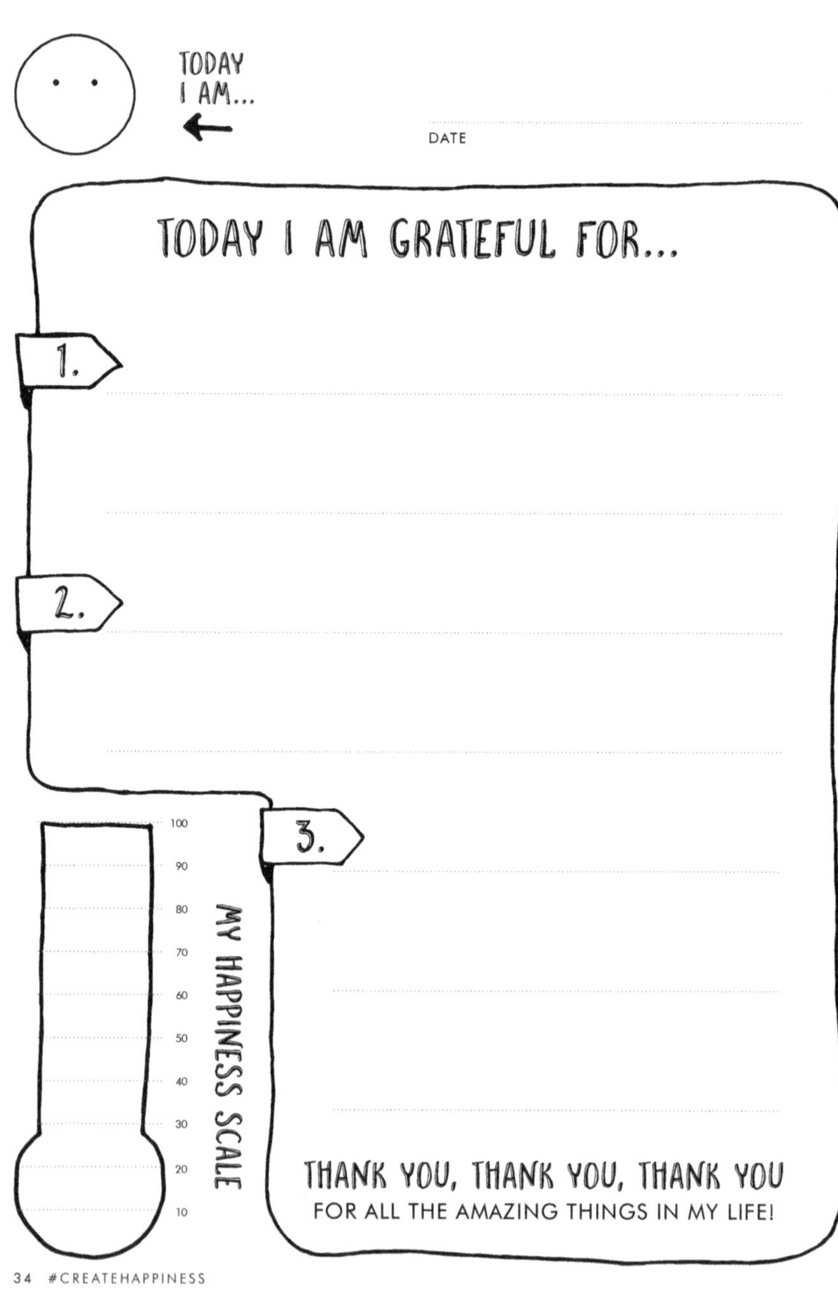

TODAY
I AM...
DATE
TODAY I AM GRATEFUL FOR...
1.
2.
3.
100
90
80
70
60
50
40
30
20
10
MY HAPPINESS SCALE
THANK YOU, THANK YOU, THANK YOU
FOR ALL THE AMAZING THINGS IN MY LIFE!

TODAY I AM GRATEFUL FOR...

1.

2.

3.

THANK YOU, THANK YOU, THANK YOU
FOR ALL THE AMAZING THINGS IN MY LIFE!

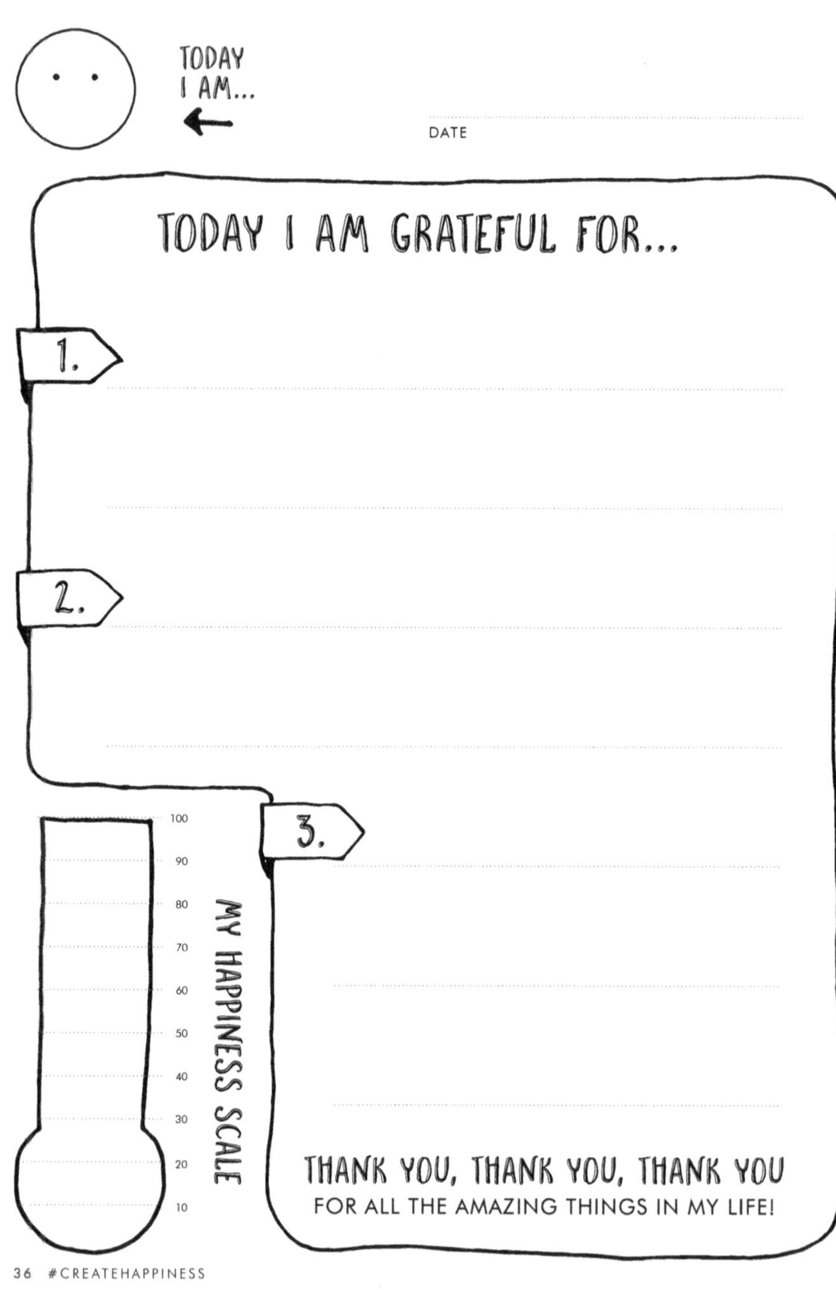

TODAY
I AM...
DATE
TODAY I AM GRATEFUL FOR...
1.
2.
3.
100
90
80
70
60
50
40
30
20
10
MY HAPPINESS SCALE
THANK YOU, THANK YOU, THANK YOU
FOR ALL THE AMAZING THINGS IN MY LIFE!

DATE

TODAY I AM GRATEFUL FOR...

1.

2.

3.

THANK YOU, THANK YOU, THANK YOU
FOR ALL THE AMAZING THINGS IN MY LIFE!

MY HAPPINESS SCALE

100
90
80
70
60
50
40
30
20
10

TODAY I AM...
DATE
TODAY I AM GRATEFUL FOR...
1.
2.
3.
MY HAPPINESS SCALE
100
90
80
70
60
50
40
30
20
10
THANK YOU, THANK YOU, THANK YOU
FOR ALL THE AMAZING THINGS IN MY LIFE!

TODAY
I AM... →

TODAY I AM GRATEFUL FOR...

1.

2.

3.

THANK YOU, THANK YOU, THANK YOU
FOR ALL THE AMAZING THINGS IN MY LIFE!

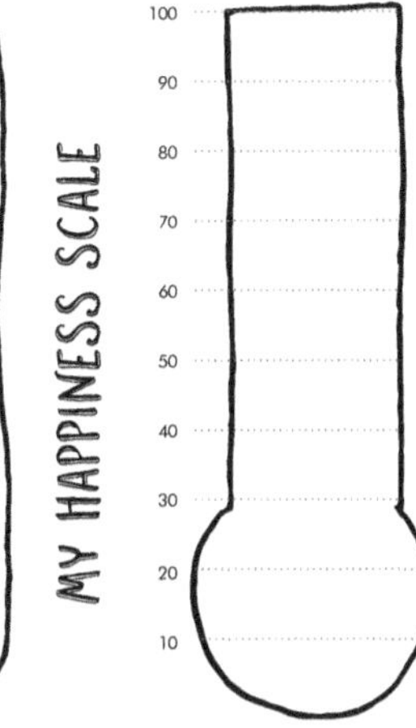

GET OUTSIDE and MOVE

HAPPINESS TIP:

Going for a walk outside, in the bush or at the beach, makes you feel more refreshed and energetic, and less tense and angry.

Exercise increases endorphines (those feel-good brain chemicals) and reduces the level of stress hormones in your body. The mood benefits of just 20 minutes of exercise can last up to 12 hours.

THINGS I LOVE TO DO
OUTSIDE

USE WORDS AND PICTURES TO DESCRIBE WHAT YOU LOVE TO DO

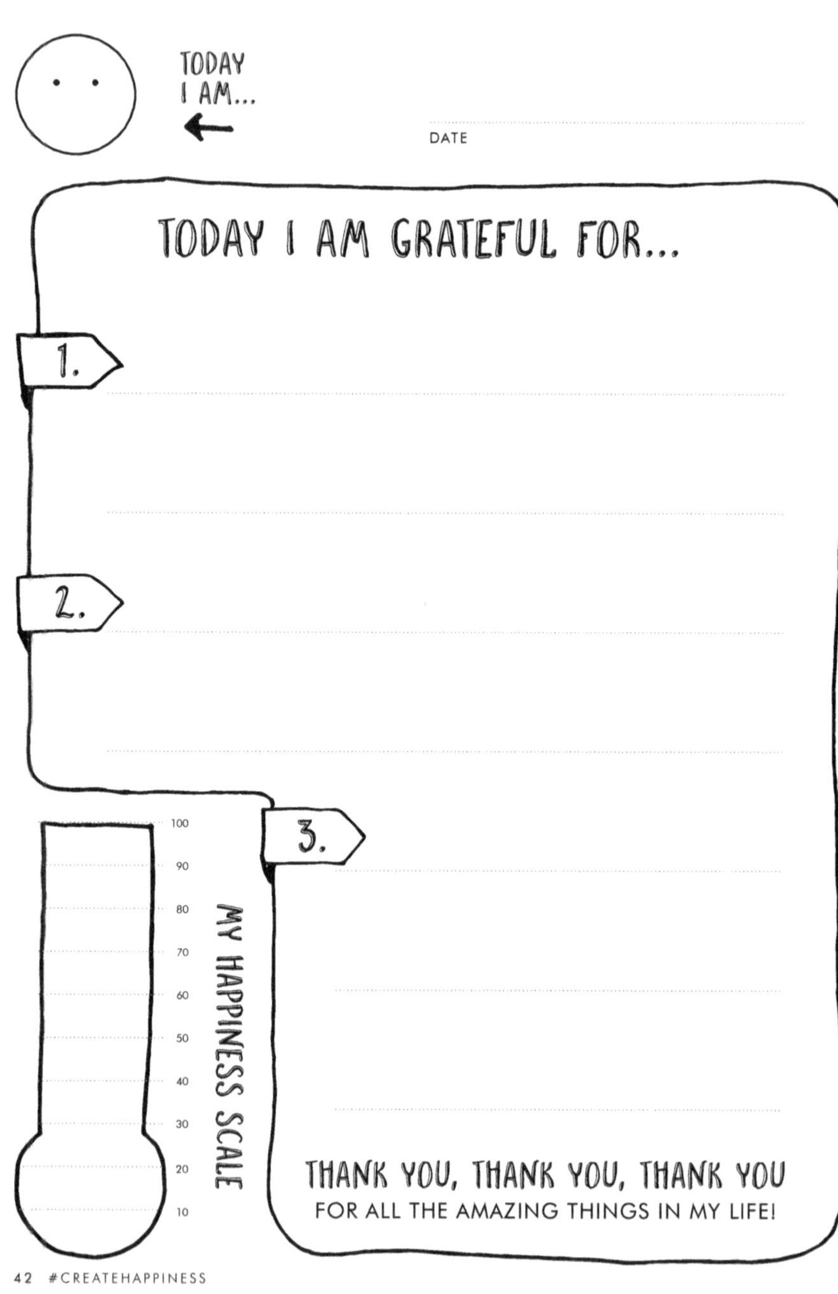

TODAY I AM...
DATE
TODAY I AM GRATEFUL FOR...
1.
2.
3.
MY HAPPINESS SCALE
100
90
80
70
60
50
40
30
20
10
THANK YOU, THANK YOU, THANK YOU
FOR ALL THE AMAZING THINGS IN MY LIFE!

DATE

TODAY I AM GRATEFUL FOR...

1.

2.

3.

THANK YOU, THANK YOU, THANK YOU
FOR ALL THE AMAZING THINGS IN MY LIFE!

MY HAPPINESS SCALE

100
90
80
70
60
50
40
30
20
10

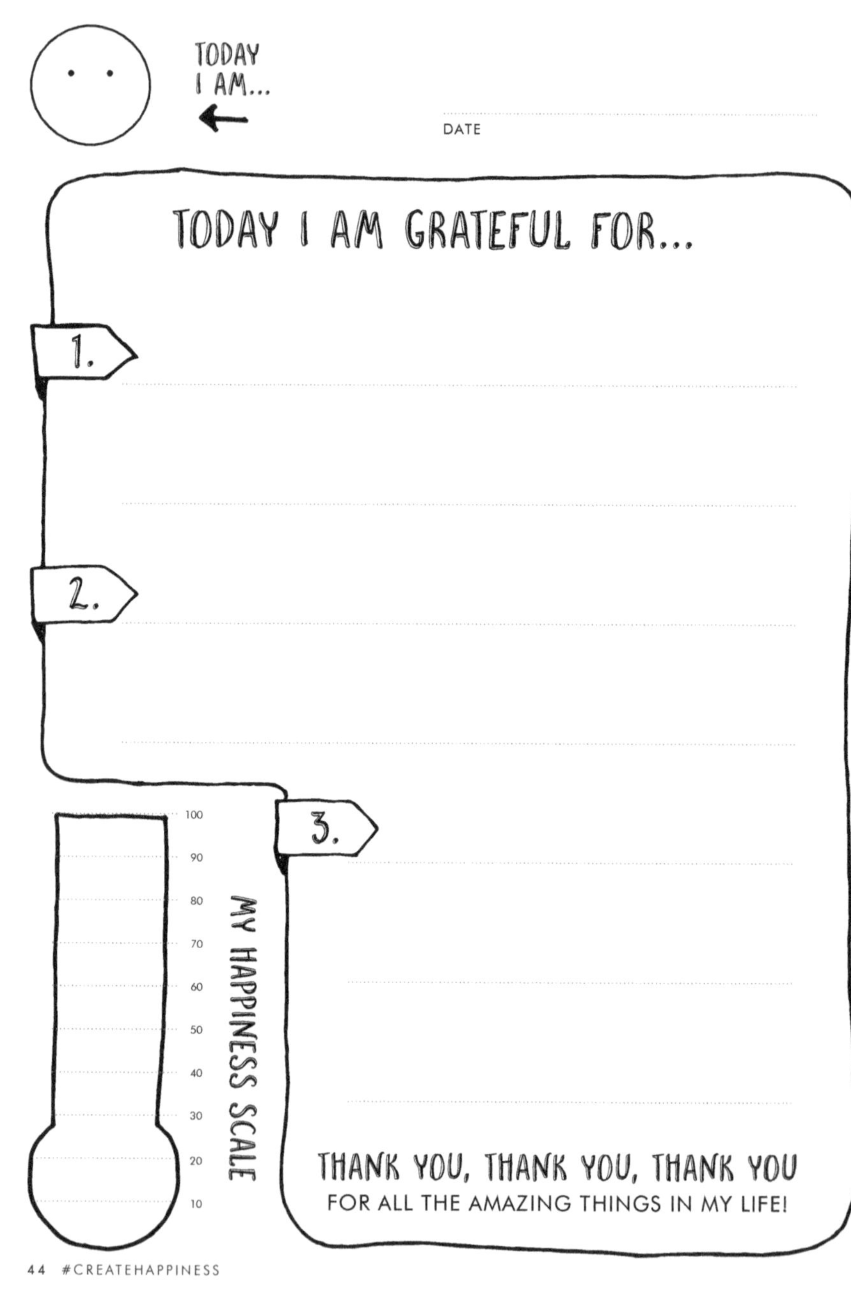

TODAY
I AM...

DATE

TODAY I AM GRATEFUL FOR...

1.

2.

3.

100
90
80
70
60
50
40
30
20
10

MY HAPPINESS SCALE

THANK YOU, THANK YOU, THANK YOU
FOR ALL THE AMAZING THINGS IN MY LIFE!

....

DATE

TODAY I AM GRATEFUL FOR...

1.

2.

3.

THANK YOU, THANK YOU, THANK YOU
FOR ALL THE AMAZING THINGS IN MY LIFE!

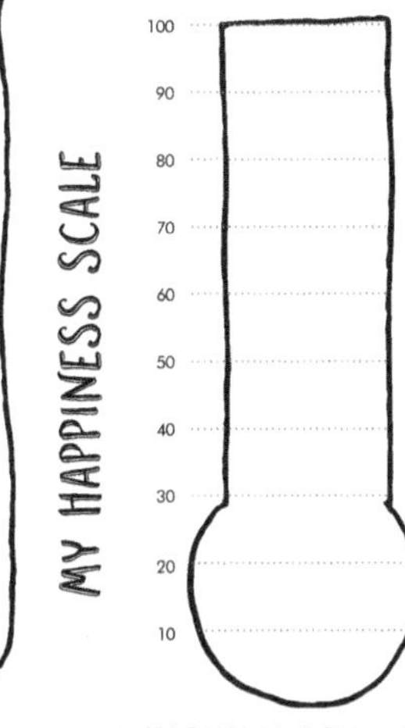

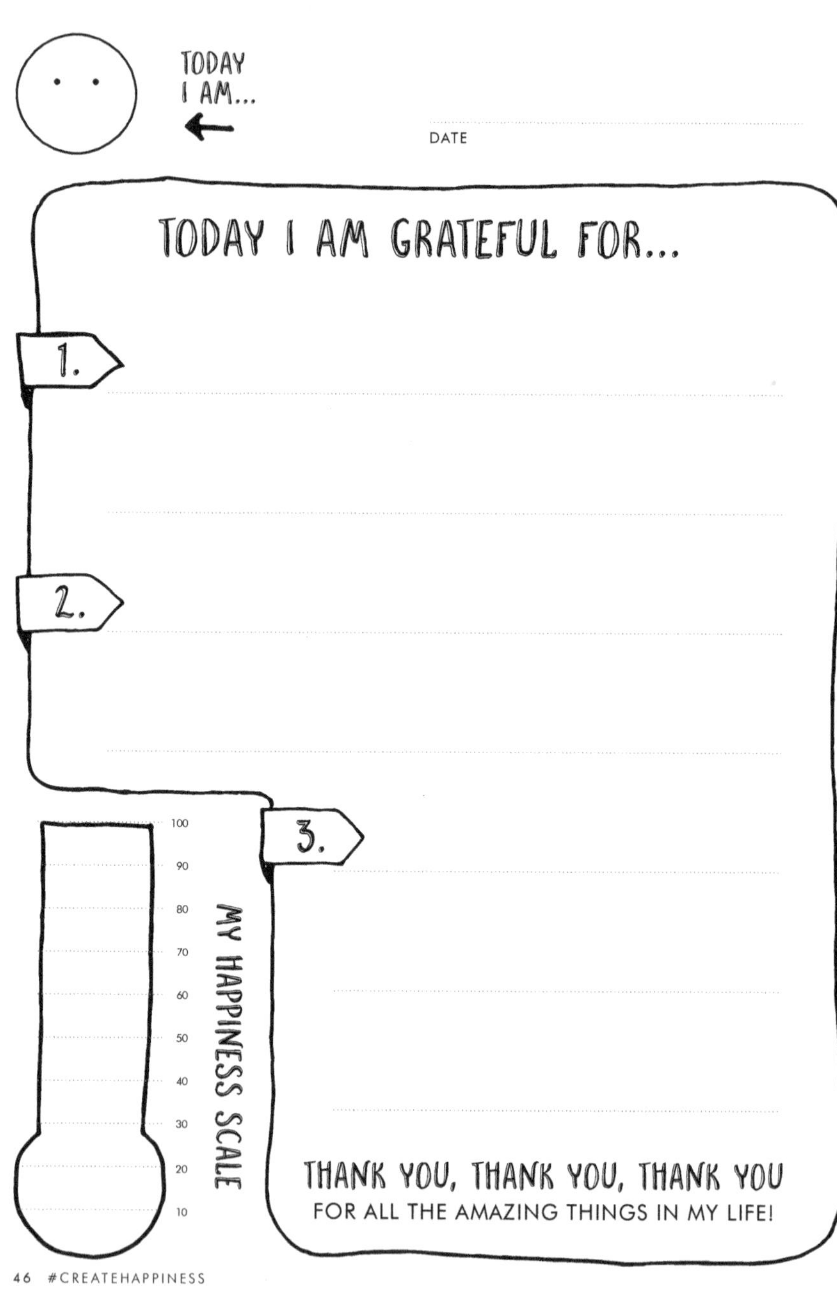

TODAY I AM...
DATE
TODAY I AM GRATEFUL FOR...
1.
2.
3.
100
90
80
70
60
50
40
30
20
10
MY HAPPINESS SCALE
THANK YOU, THANK YOU, THANK YOU
FOR ALL THE AMAZING THINGS IN MY LIFE!

TODAY
I AM...
→

TODAY I AM GRATEFUL FOR...

1.

2.

3.

THANK YOU, THANK YOU, THANK YOU
FOR ALL THE AMAZING THINGS IN MY LIFE!

MY HAPPINESS SCALE

100
90
80
70
60
50
40
30
20
10

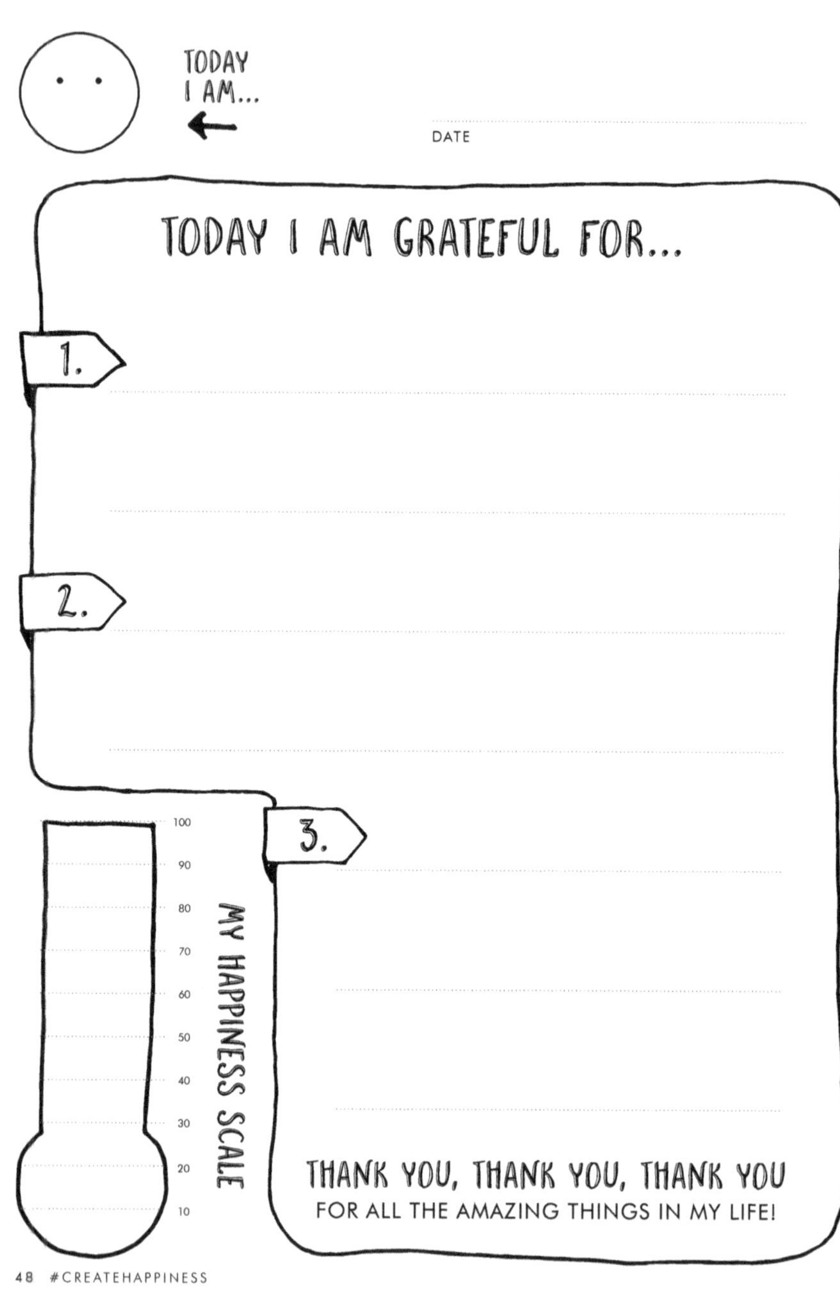
TODAY I AM...
DATE
TODAY I AM GRATEFUL FOR...
1.
2.
3.
100
90
80
70
60
50
40
30
20
10
MY HAPPINESS SCALE
THANK YOU, THANK YOU, THANK YOU
FOR ALL THE AMAZING THINGS IN MY LIFE!

DATE

TODAY I AM GRATEFUL FOR...

1.

2.

3.

THANK YOU, THANK YOU, THANK YOU
FOR ALL THE AMAZING THINGS IN MY LIFE!

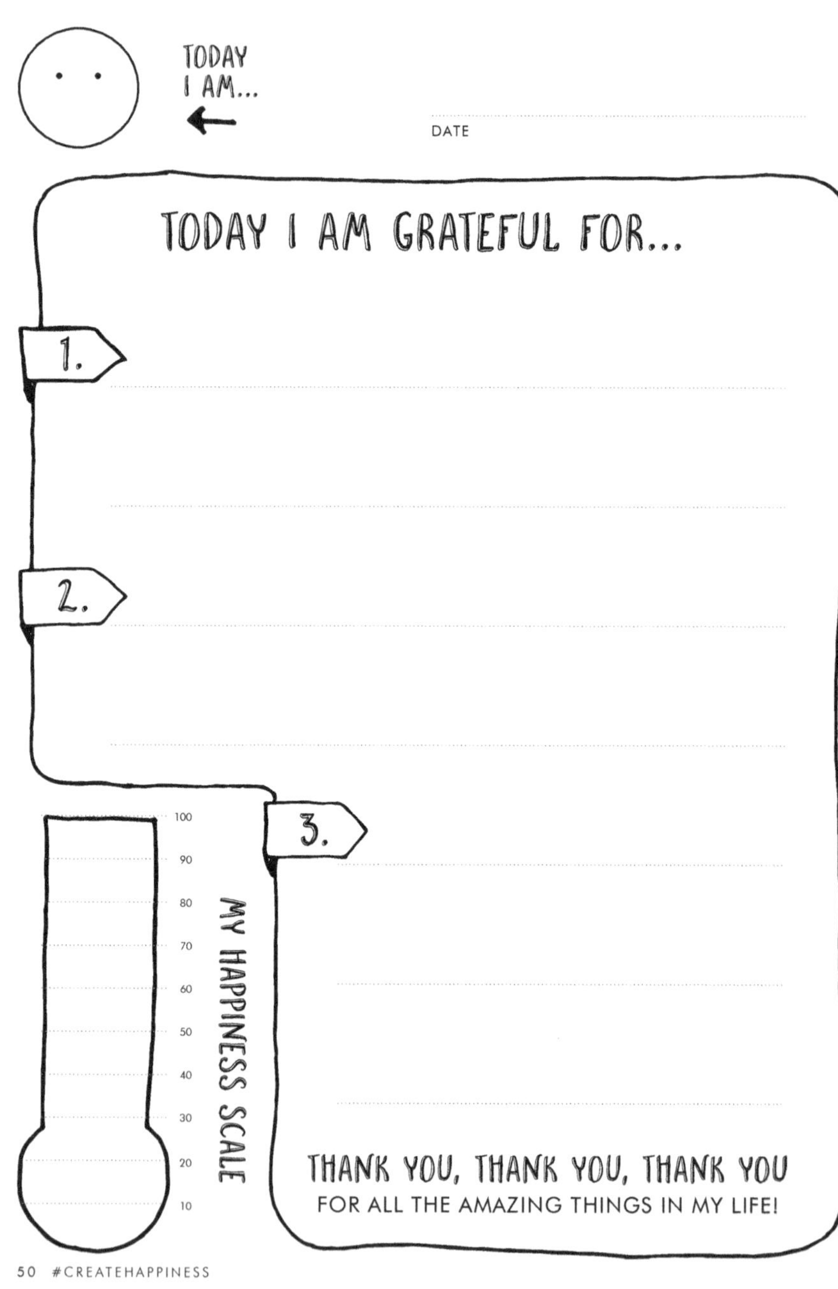

TODAY
I AM...
DATE
TODAY I AM GRATEFUL FOR...
1.
2.
3.
100
90
80
70
60
50
40
30
20
10
MY HAPPINESS SCALE
THANK YOU, THANK YOU, THANK YOU
FOR ALL THE AMAZING THINGS IN MY LIFE!

DRAWING BY ARABELLA, AGE 7

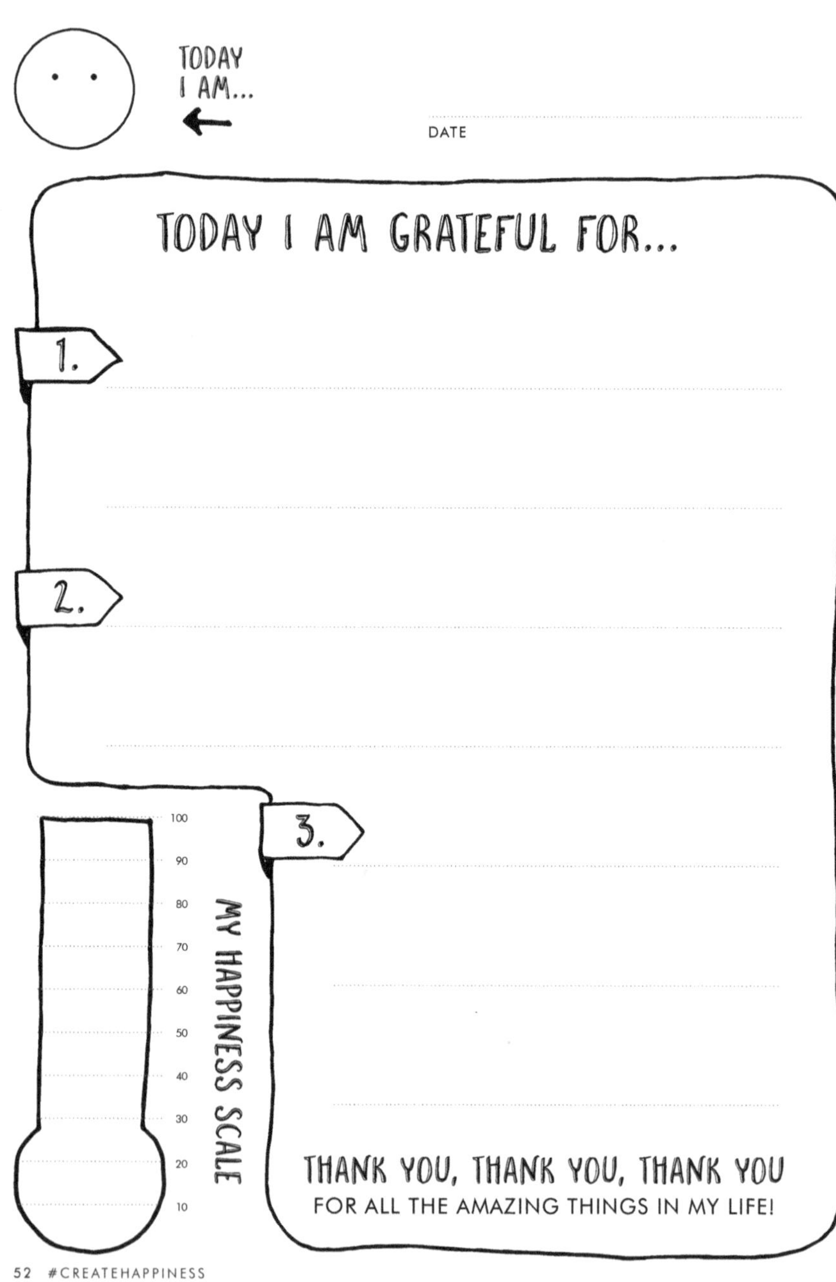

TODAY I AM...
DATE
TODAY I AM GRATEFUL FOR...
1.
2.
3.
MY HAPPINESS SCALE
100
90
80
70
60
50
40
30
20
10
THANK YOU, THANK YOU, THANK YOU
FOR ALL THE AMAZING THINGS IN MY LIFE!

DATE

TODAY I AM GRATEFUL FOR...

1.

2.

3.

THANK YOU, THANK YOU, THANK YOU
FOR ALL THE AMAZING THINGS IN MY LIFE!

MY HAPPINESS SCALE

100
90
80
70
60
50
40
30
20
10

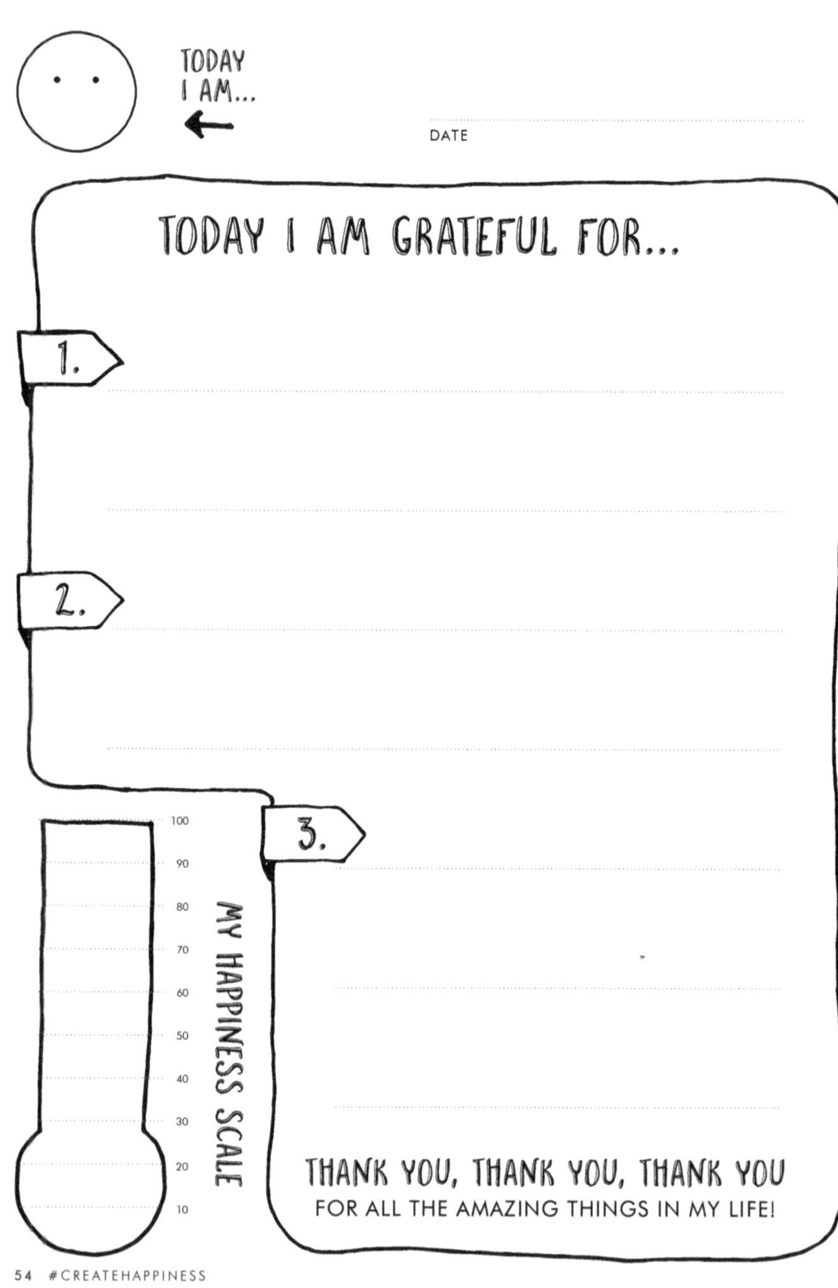

TODAY
I AM...

DATE

TODAY I AM GRATEFUL FOR...

1.

2.

3.

MY HAPPINESS SCALE

100
90
80
70
60
50
40
30
20
10

THANK YOU, THANK YOU, THANK YOU
FOR ALL THE AMAZING THINGS IN MY LIFE!

DATE

TODAY I AM GRATEFUL FOR...

1.

2.

3.

THANK YOU, THANK YOU, THANK YOU
FOR ALL THE AMAZING THINGS IN MY LIFE!

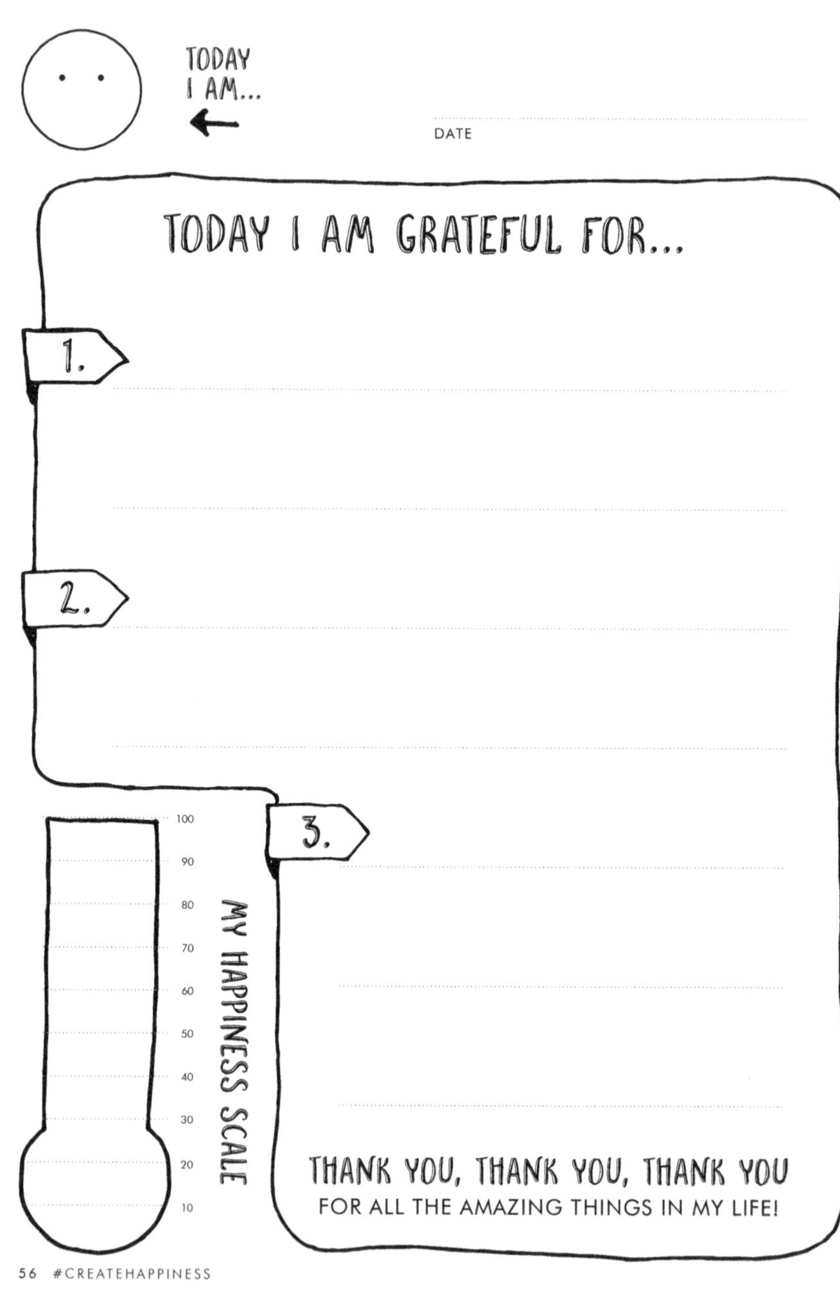

TODAY I AM...
DATE
TODAY I AM GRATEFUL FOR...
1.
2.
3.
100
90
80
70
60
50
40
30
20
10
MY HAPPINESS SCALE
THANK YOU, THANK YOU, THANK YOU
FOR ALL THE AMAZING THINGS IN MY LIFE!

TODAY
I AM...
→

TODAY I AM GRATEFUL FOR...

1.

2.

3.

THANK YOU, THANK YOU, THANK YOU
FOR ALL THE AMAZING THINGS IN MY LIFE!

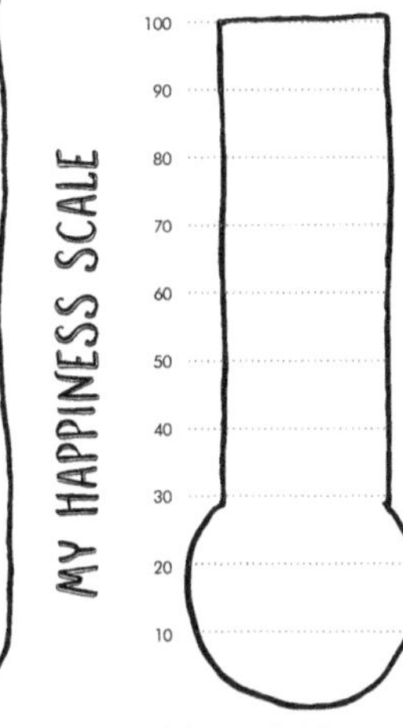

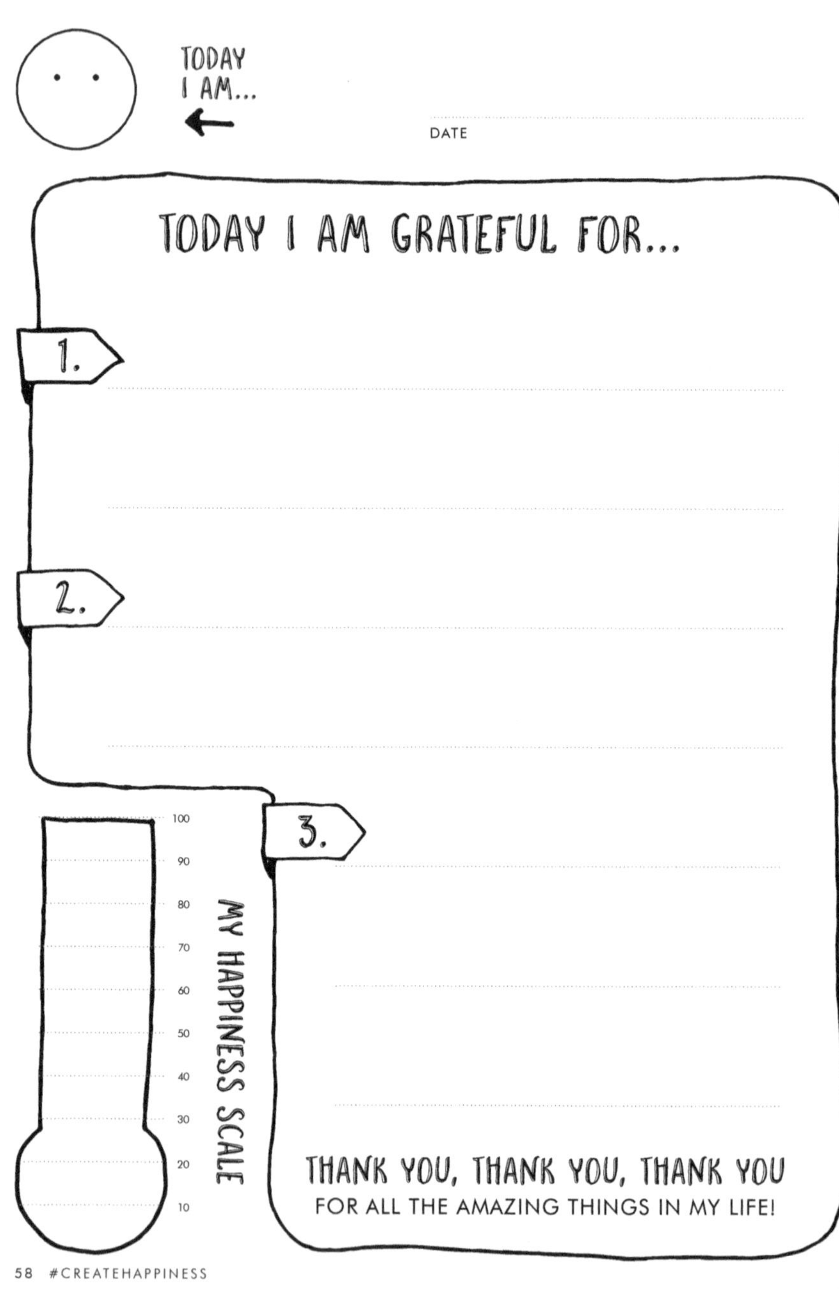

TODAY I AM...
DATE
TODAY I AM GRATEFUL FOR...
1.
2.
3.
MY HAPPINESS SCALE
100
90
80
70
60
50
40
30
20
10
THANK YOU, THANK YOU, THANK YOU
FOR ALL THE AMAZING THINGS IN MY LIFE!

TODAY
I AM... →

TODAY I AM GRATEFUL FOR...

1.

2.

3.

THANK YOU, THANK YOU, THANK YOU
FOR ALL THE AMAZING THINGS IN MY LIFE!

MY HAPPINESS SCALE →

100
90
80
70
60
50
40
30
20
10

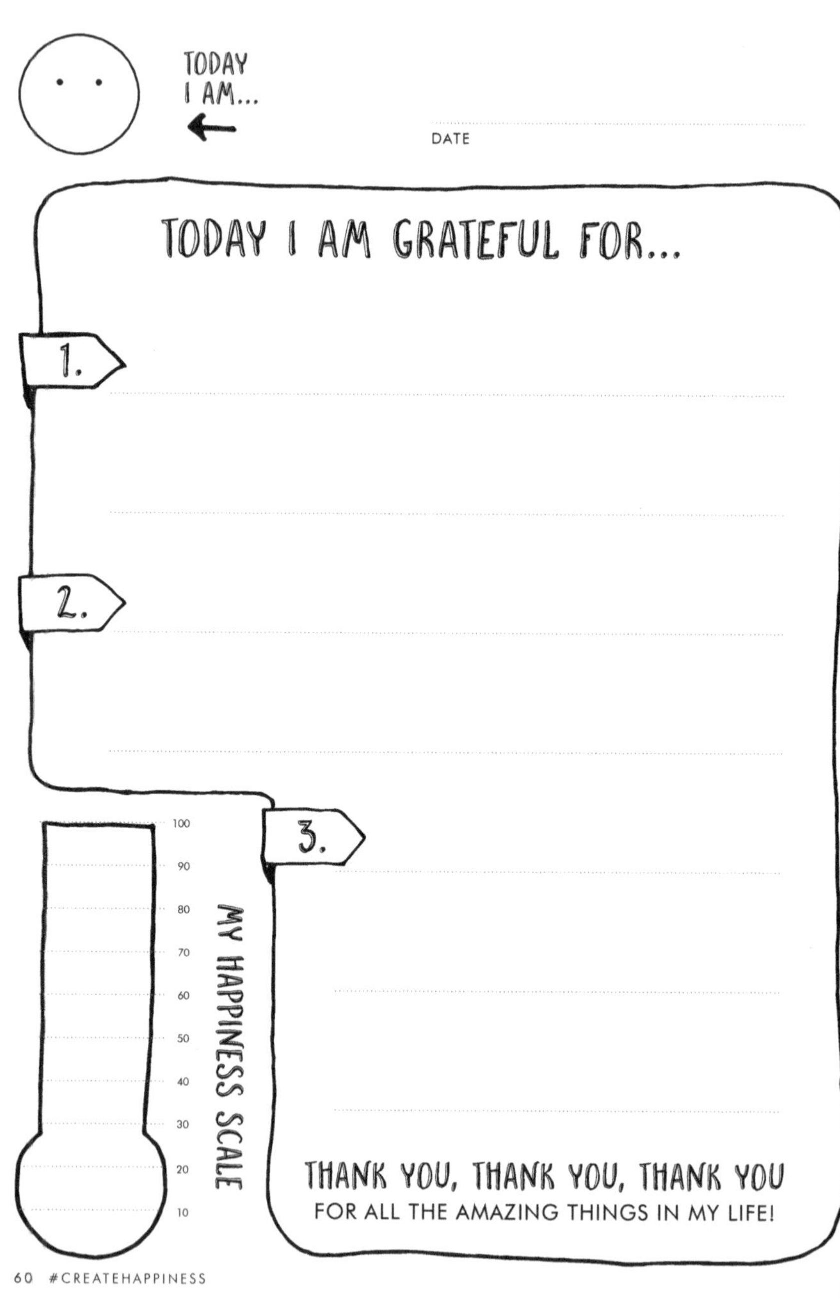

TODAY I AM GRATEFUL FOR...

SOMETHING AWESOME
THAT HAPPENED TO ME

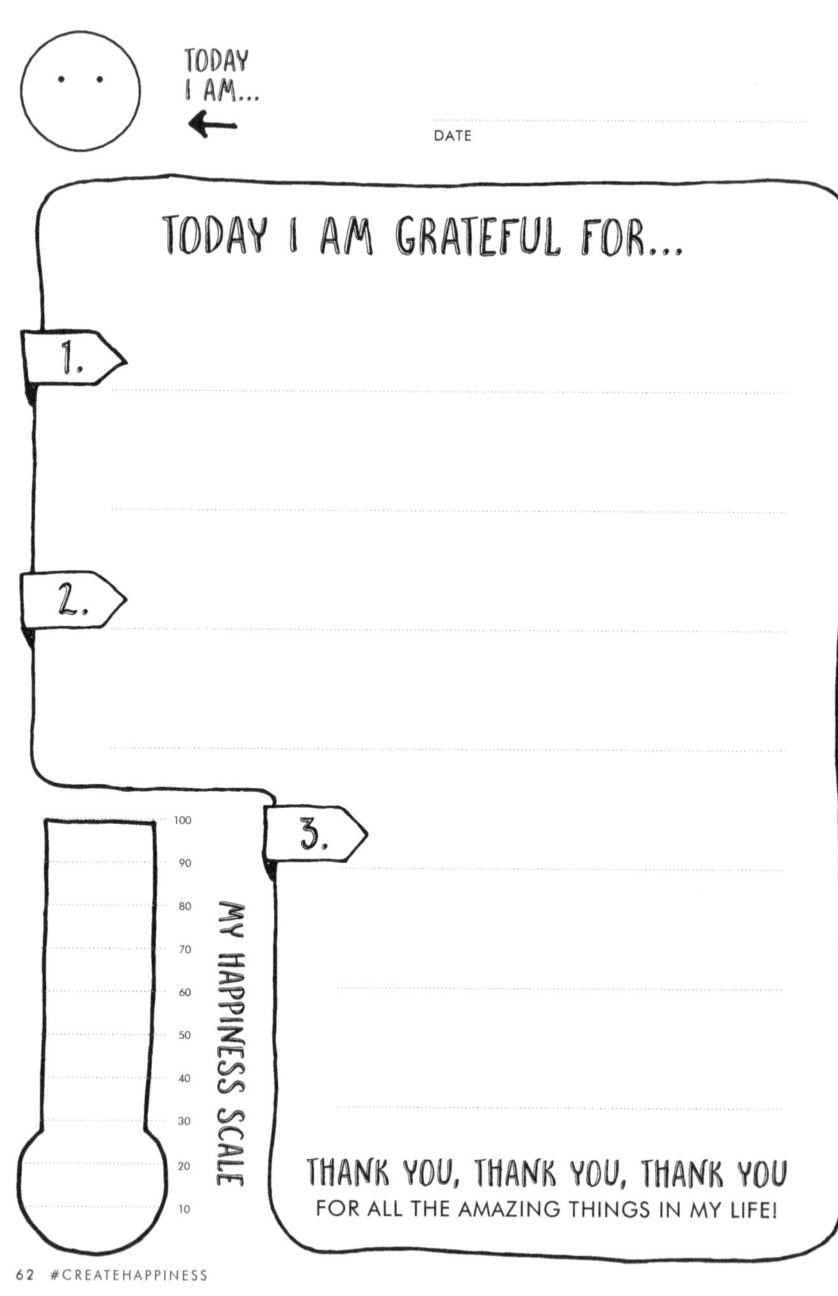

TODAY I AM...
DATE
TODAY I AM GRATEFUL FOR...
1.
2.
3.
100
90
80
70
60
50
40
30
20
10
MY HAPPINESS SCALE
THANK YOU, THANK YOU, THANK YOU
FOR ALL THE AMAZING THINGS IN MY LIFE!

....
DATE

TODAY I AM GRATEFUL FOR...

1.

2.

3.

THANK YOU, THANK YOU, THANK YOU
FOR ALL THE AMAZING THINGS IN MY LIFE!

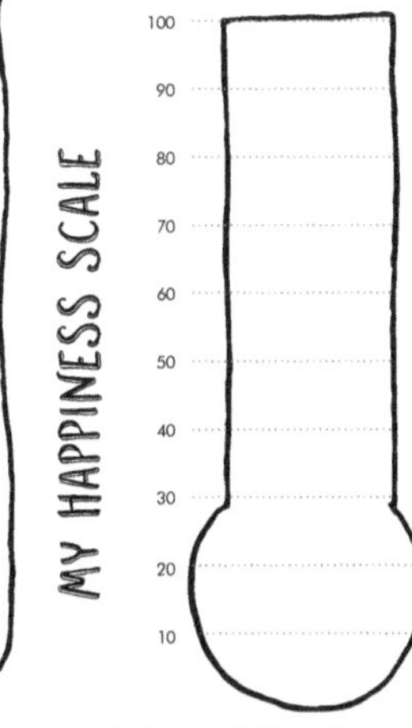

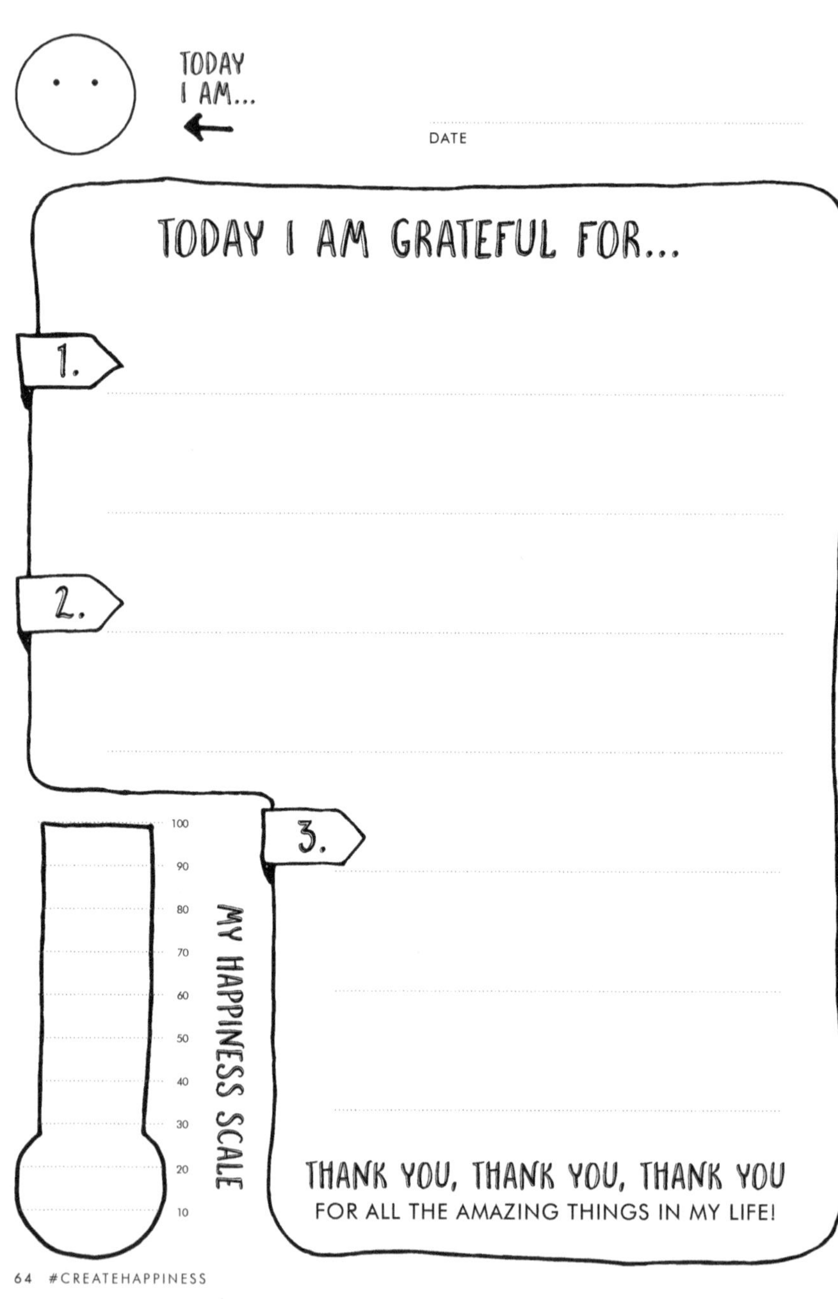
TODAY I AM...
DATE
TODAY I AM GRATEFUL FOR...
1.
2.
3.
100
90
80
70
60
50
40
30
20
10
MY HAPPINESS SCALE
THANK YOU, THANK YOU, THANK YOU
FOR ALL THE AMAZING THINGS IN MY LIFE!

DATE

TODAY I AM GRATEFUL FOR...

1.

2.

3.

THANK YOU, THANK YOU, THANK YOU
FOR ALL THE AMAZING THINGS IN MY LIFE!

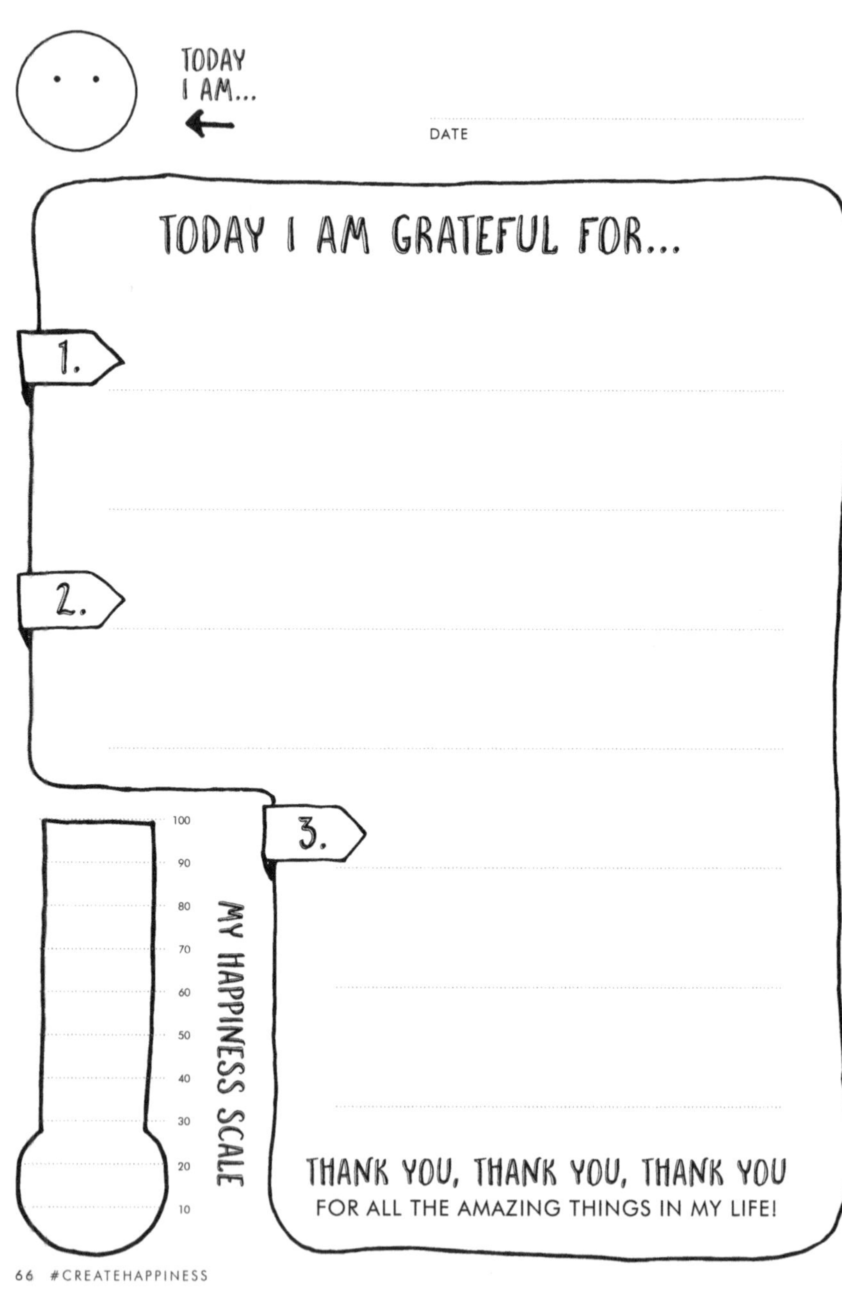

TODAY
I AM...
DATE
TODAY I AM GRATEFUL FOR...
1.
2.
3.
100
90
80
70
60
50
40
30
20
10
MY HAPPINESS SCALE
THANK YOU, THANK YOU, THANK YOU
FOR ALL THE AMAZING THINGS IN MY LIFE!

DATE

TODAY I AM GRATEFUL FOR...

1.

2.

3.

THANK YOU, THANK YOU, THANK YOU
FOR ALL THE AMAZING THINGS IN MY LIFE!

MY HAPPINESS SCALE

100
90
80
70
60
50
40
30
20
10

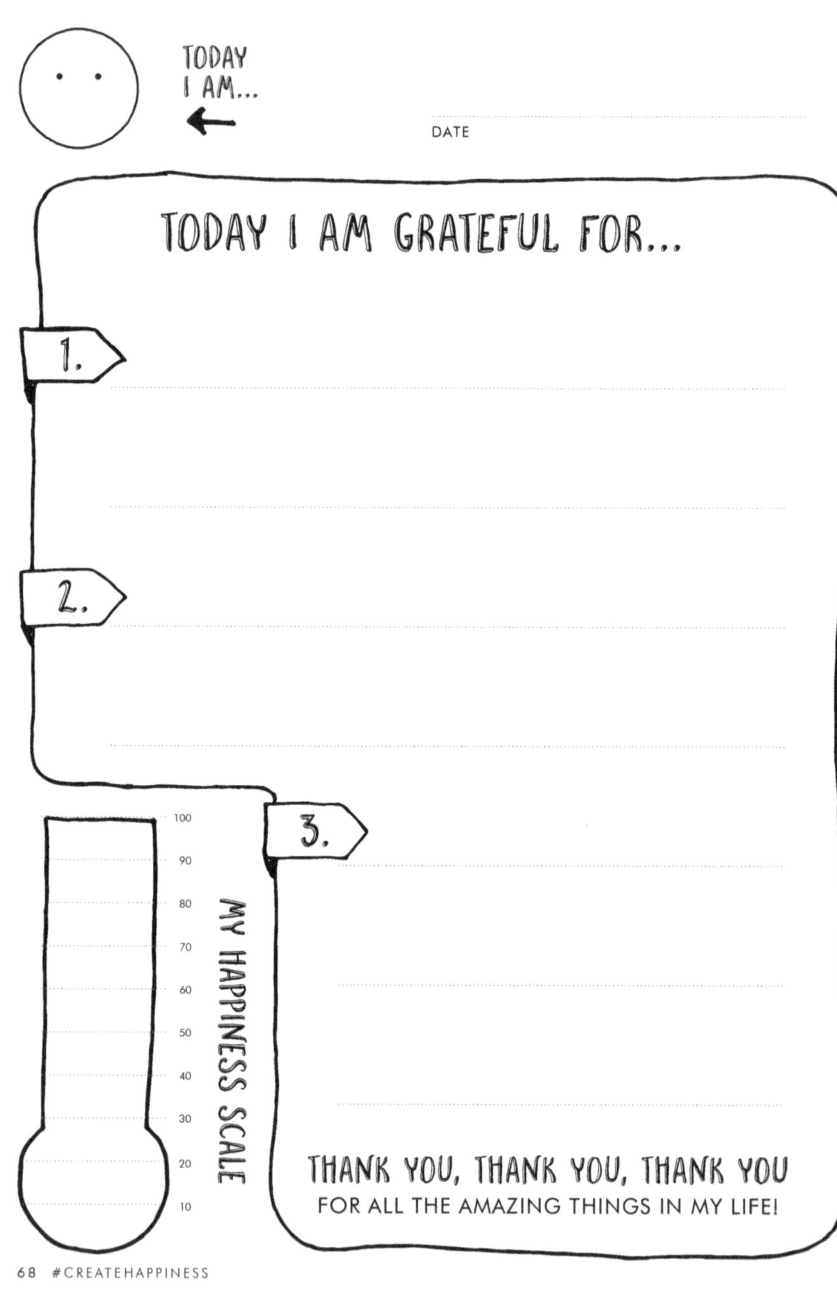

TODAY
I AM...
DATE
TODAY I AM GRATEFUL FOR...
1.
2.
3.
100
90
80
70
60
50
40
30
20
10
MY HAPPINESS SCALE
THANK YOU, THANK YOU, THANK YOU
FOR ALL THE AMAZING THINGS IN MY LIFE!

....
DATE

TODAY I AM GRATEFUL FOR...

1.

2.

3.

THANK YOU, THANK YOU, THANK YOU
FOR ALL THE AMAZING THINGS IN MY LIFE!

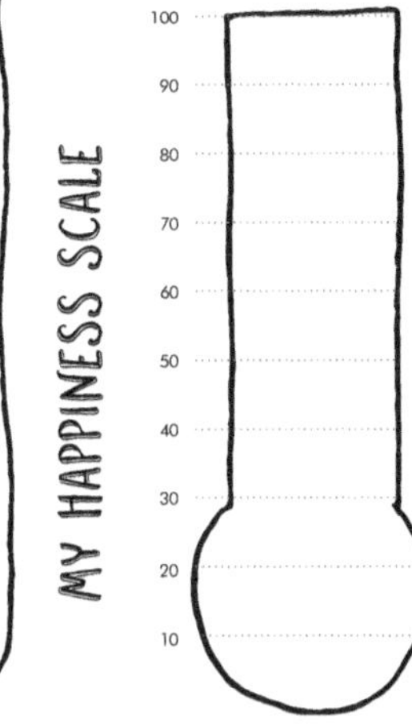

HAPPINESS IS CONTAGIOUS

HAPPINESS TIP:

We are all connected, so what we feel affects the people around us. Smile at at stranger you pass on the street. If you make eye contact, they will likely smile back. You just made them happy too!

Did you know smiling may increase your lifespan, lower stress hormones and blood pressure. The muscles in your face send messages that alter the area of the brain that affect emotions. Smiling actually stimulates those feel-good areas of the brain more than chocolate and money.

THINGS THAT MAKE ME HAPPY!

USE WORDS AND PICTURES TO DESCRIBE WHAT MAKES YOU HAPPY

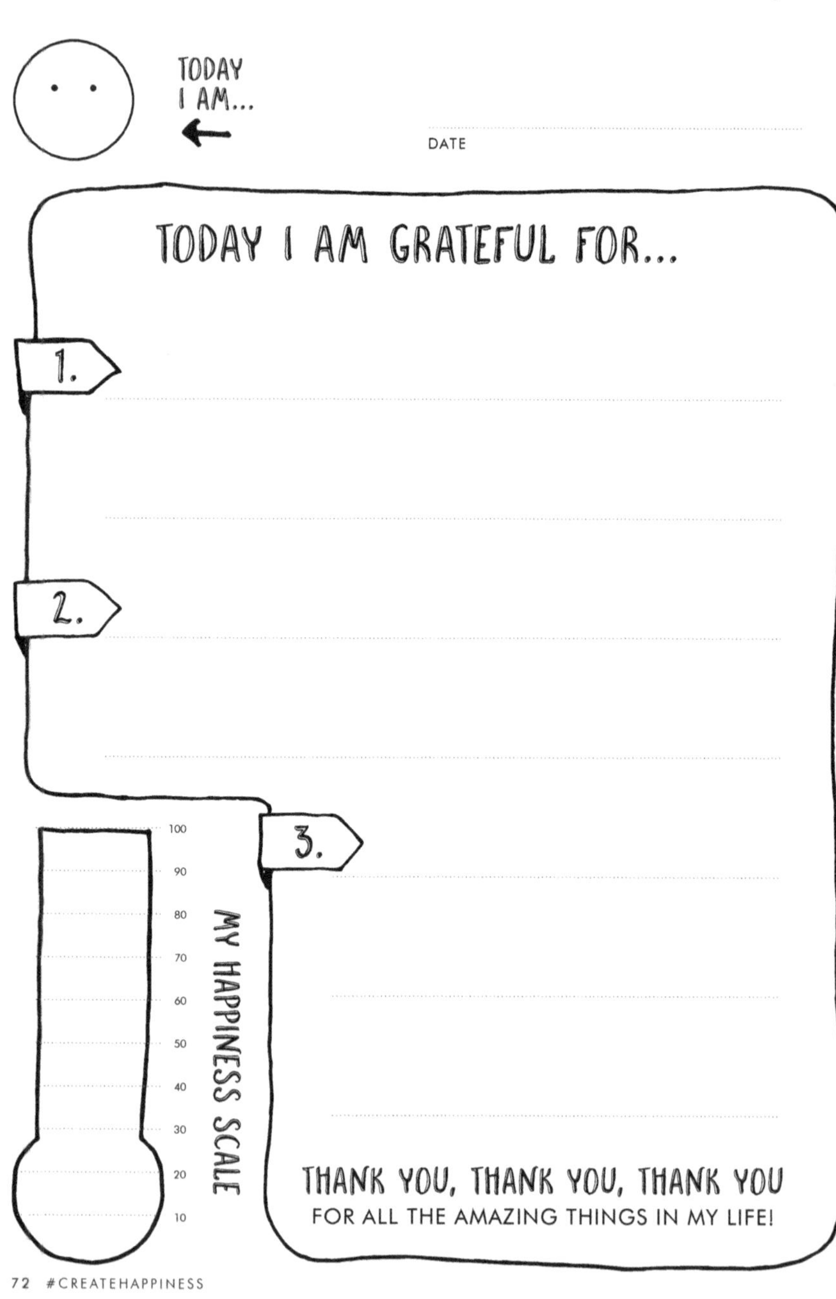

TODAY
I AM...

DATE

TODAY I AM GRATEFUL FOR...

1.

2.

3.

100
90
80
70
60
50
40
30
20
10

MY HAPPINESS SCALE

THANK YOU, THANK YOU, THANK YOU
FOR ALL THE AMAZING THINGS IN MY LIFE!

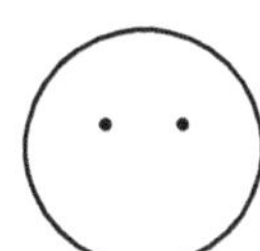

TODAY I AM GRATEFUL FOR...

1.

2.

3.

THANK YOU, THANK YOU, THANK YOU
FOR ALL THE AMAZING THINGS IN MY LIFE!

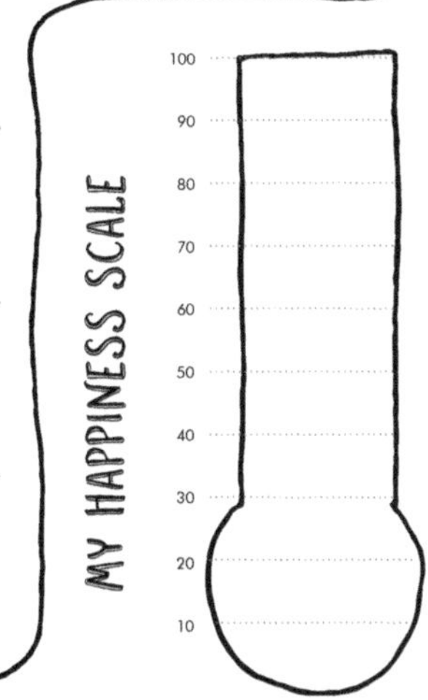

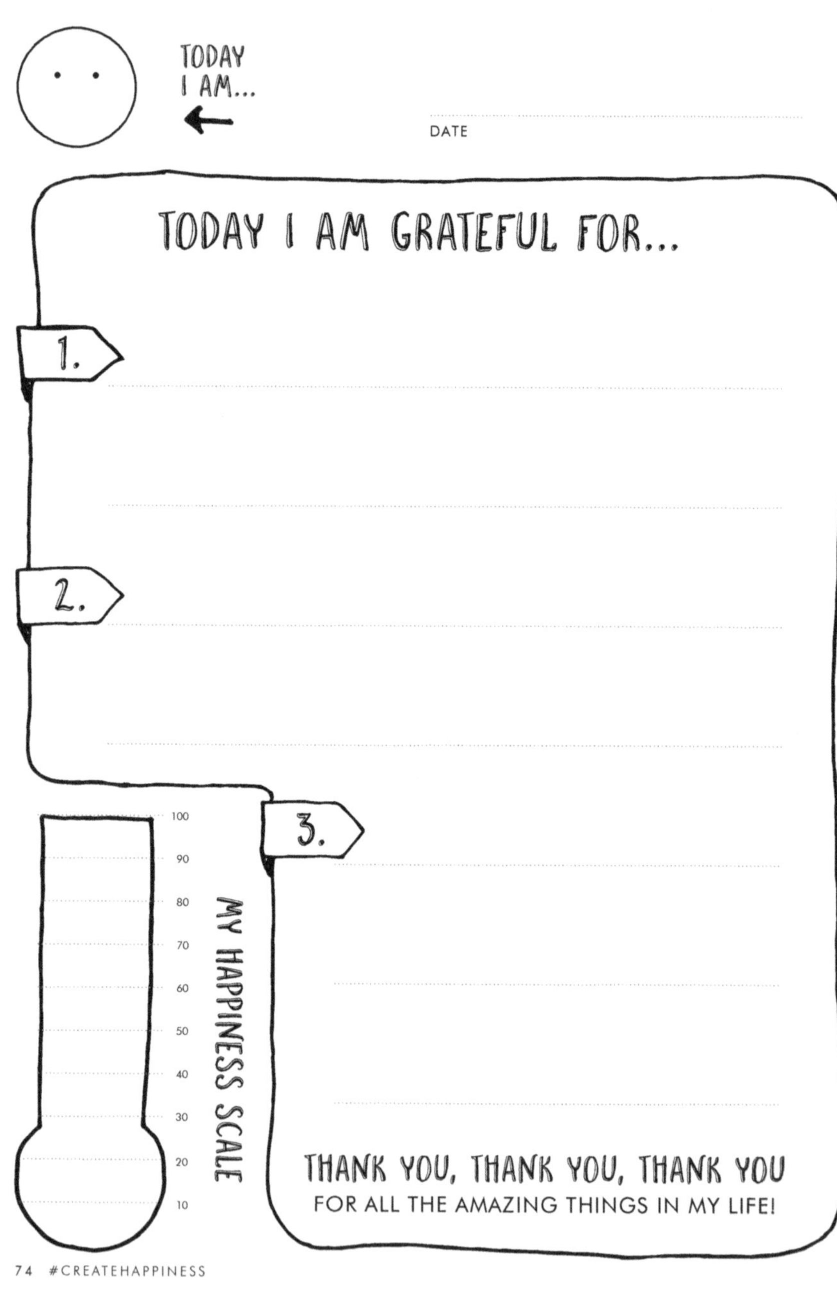
TODAY
I AM...

DATE

TODAY I AM GRATEFUL FOR...

1.

2.

3.

100
90
80
70
60
50
40
30
20
10

MY HAPPINESS SCALE

THANK YOU, THANK YOU, THANK YOU
FOR ALL THE AMAZING THINGS IN MY LIFE!

TODAY I AM... →

TODAY I AM GRATEFUL FOR...

1.

2.

3.

THANK YOU, THANK YOU, THANK YOU
FOR ALL THE AMAZING THINGS IN MY LIFE!

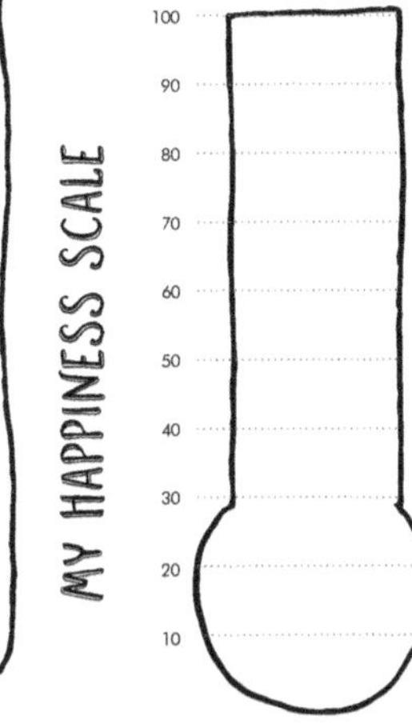

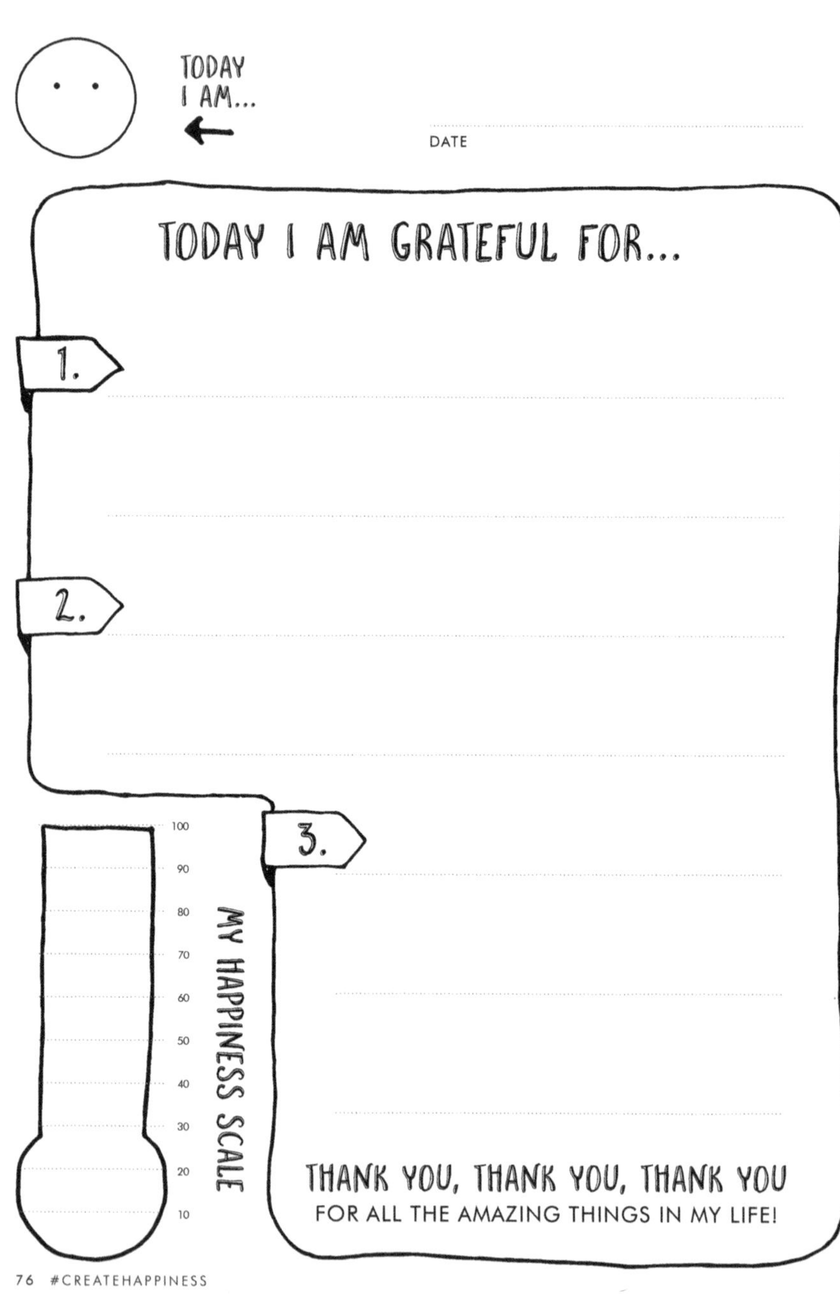

TODAY I AM...
DATE
TODAY I AM GRATEFUL FOR...
1.
2.
3.
100
90
80
70
60
50
40
30
20
10
MY HAPPINESS SCALE
THANK YOU, THANK YOU, THANK YOU
FOR ALL THE AMAZING THINGS IN MY LIFE!

DATE

TODAY I AM GRATEFUL FOR...

1.

2.

3.

THANK YOU, THANK YOU, THANK YOU
FOR ALL THE AMAZING THINGS IN MY LIFE!

MY HAPPINESS SCALE

100
90
80
70
60
50
40
30
20
10

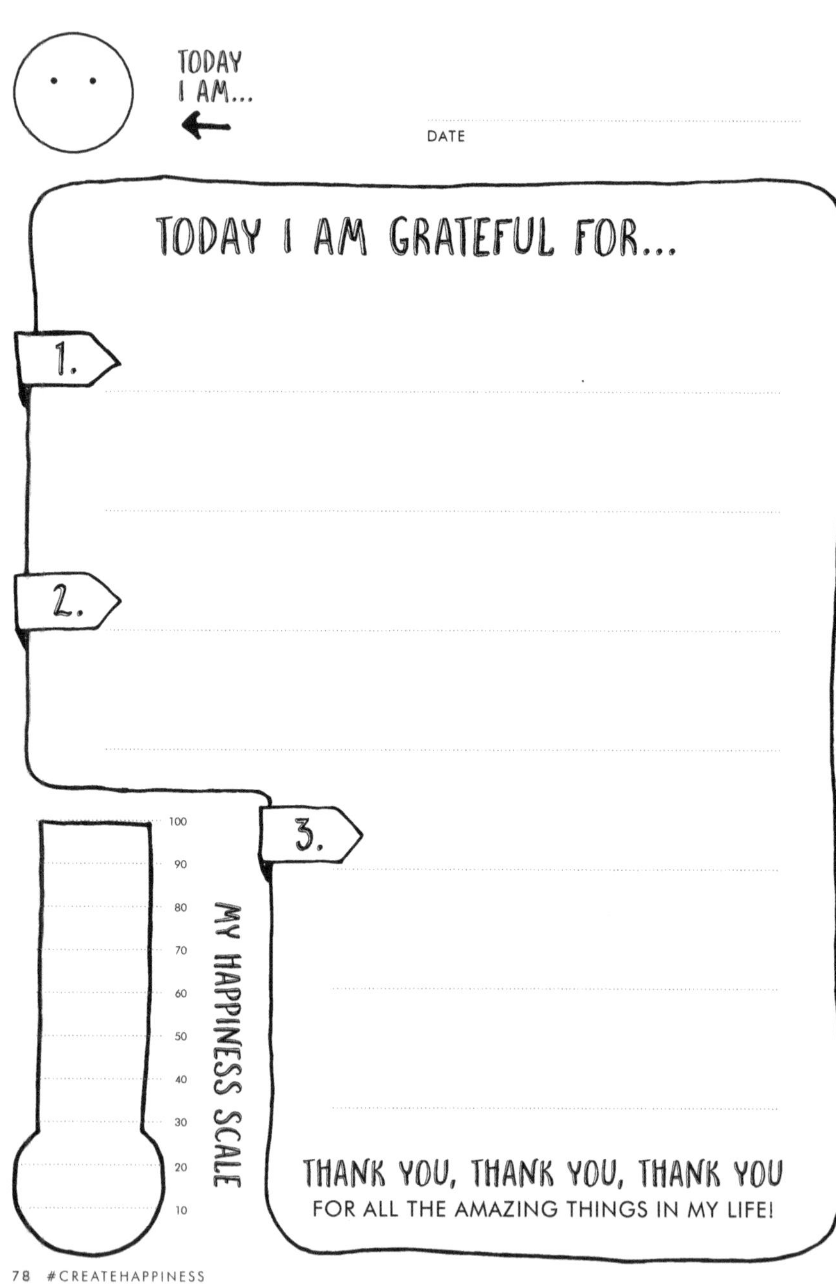

TODAY
I AM...
DATE
TODAY I AM GRATEFUL FOR...
1.
2.
3.
100
90
80
70
60
50
40
30
20
10
MY HAPPINESS SCALE
THANK YOU, THANK YOU, THANK YOU
FOR ALL THE AMAZING THINGS IN MY LIFE!

DATE

TODAY I AM GRATEFUL FOR...

1.

2.

3.

MY HAPPINESS SCALE

100
90
80
70
60
50
40
30
20
10

THANK YOU, THANK YOU, THANK YOU
FOR ALL THE AMAZING THINGS IN MY LIFE!

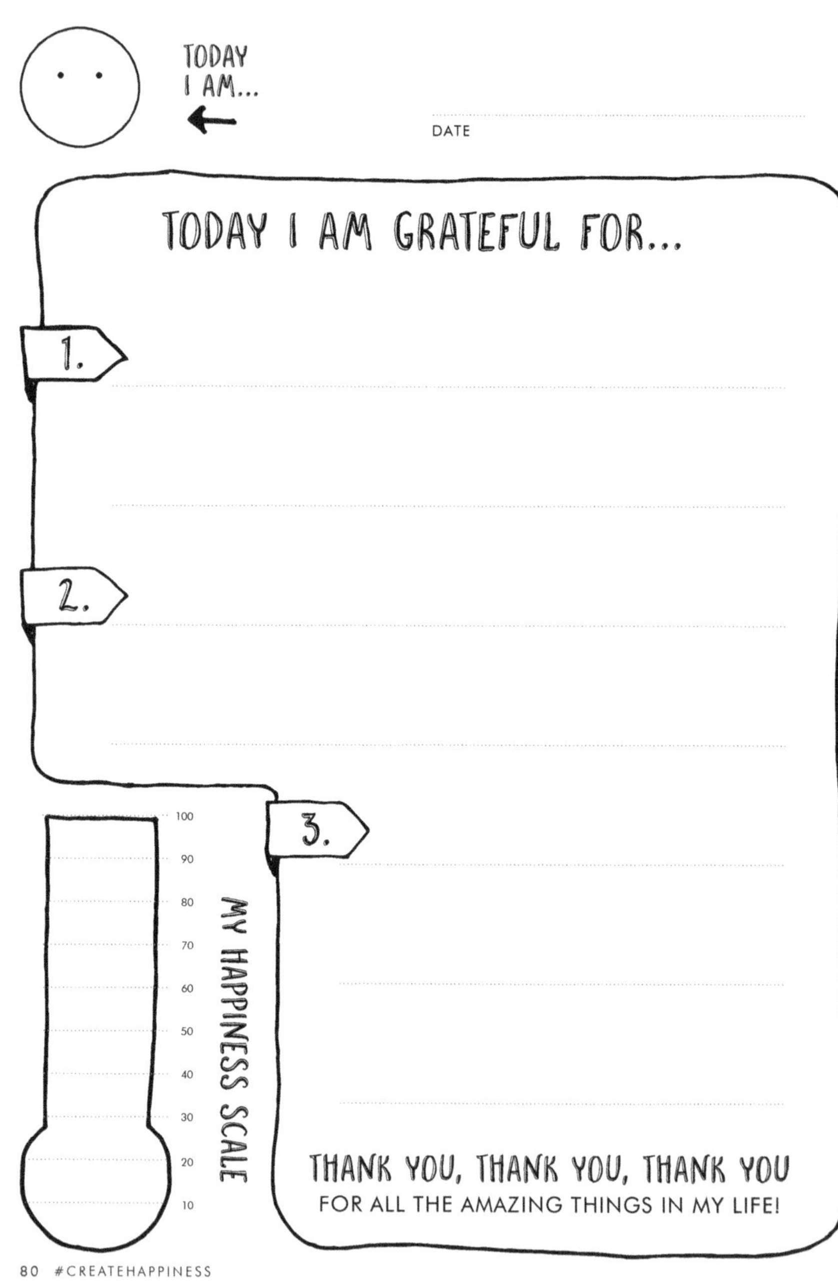

TODAY I AM...
DATE
TODAY I AM GRATEFUL FOR...
1.
2.
3.
100
90
80
70
60
50
40
30
20
10
MY HAPPINESS SCALE
THANK YOU, THANK YOU, THANK YOU
FOR ALL THE AMAZING THINGS IN MY LIFE!

DRAWING BY KELLY, AGE 14

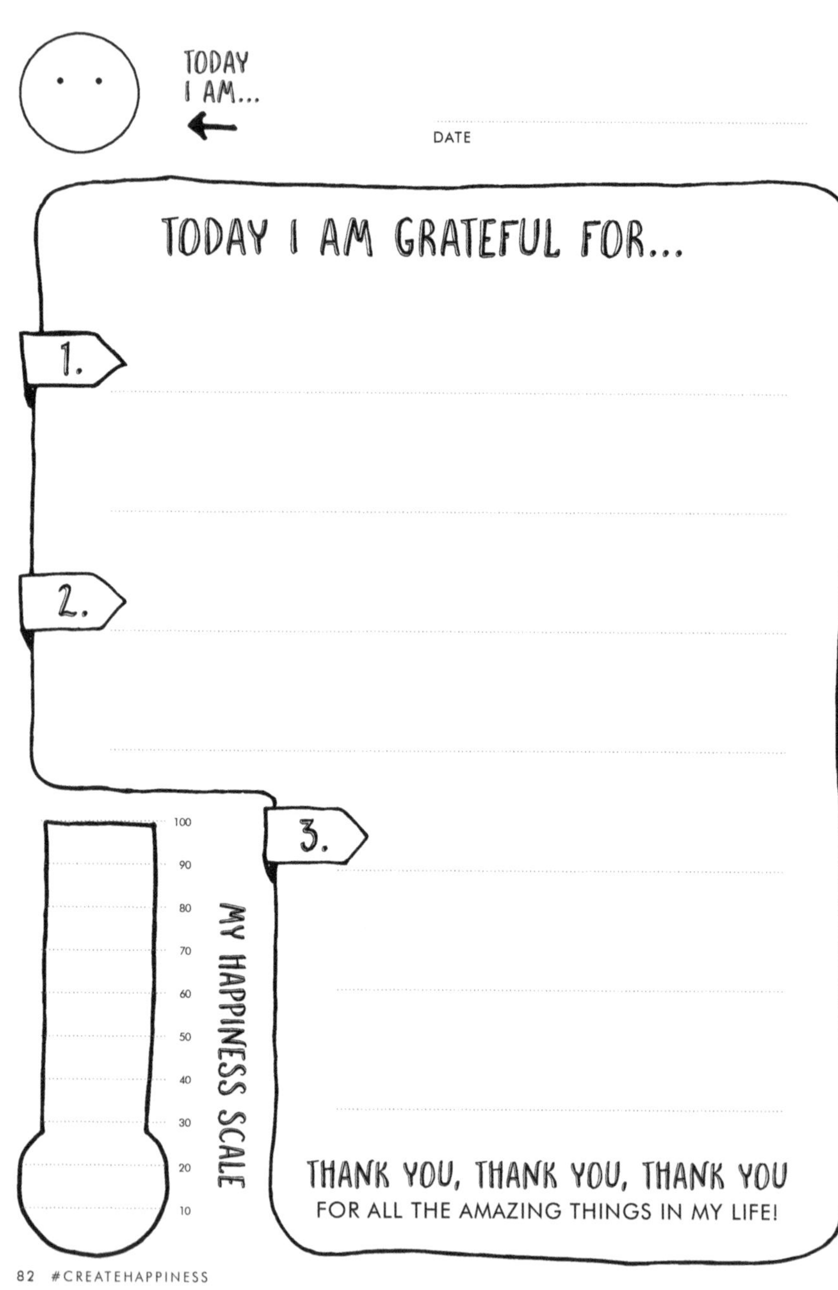

TODAY
I AM...
DATE
TODAY I AM GRATEFUL FOR...
1.
2.
3.
100
90
80
70
60
50
40
30
20
10
MY HAPPINESS SCALE
THANK YOU, THANK YOU, THANK YOU
FOR ALL THE AMAZING THINGS IN MY LIFE!

DATE

TODAY I AM GRATEFUL FOR...

1.

2.

3.

THANK YOU, THANK YOU, THANK YOU
FOR ALL THE AMAZING THINGS IN MY LIFE!

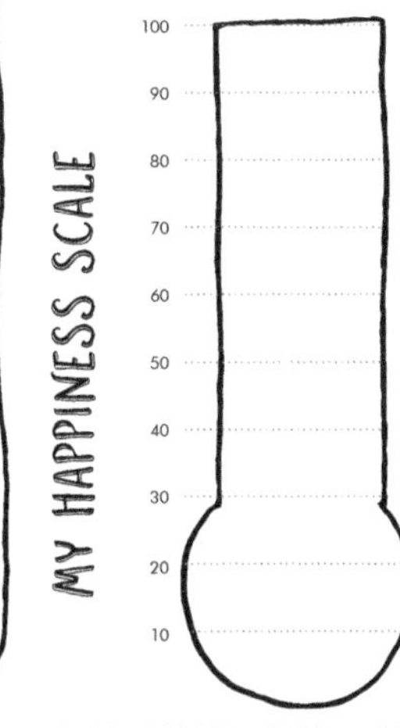

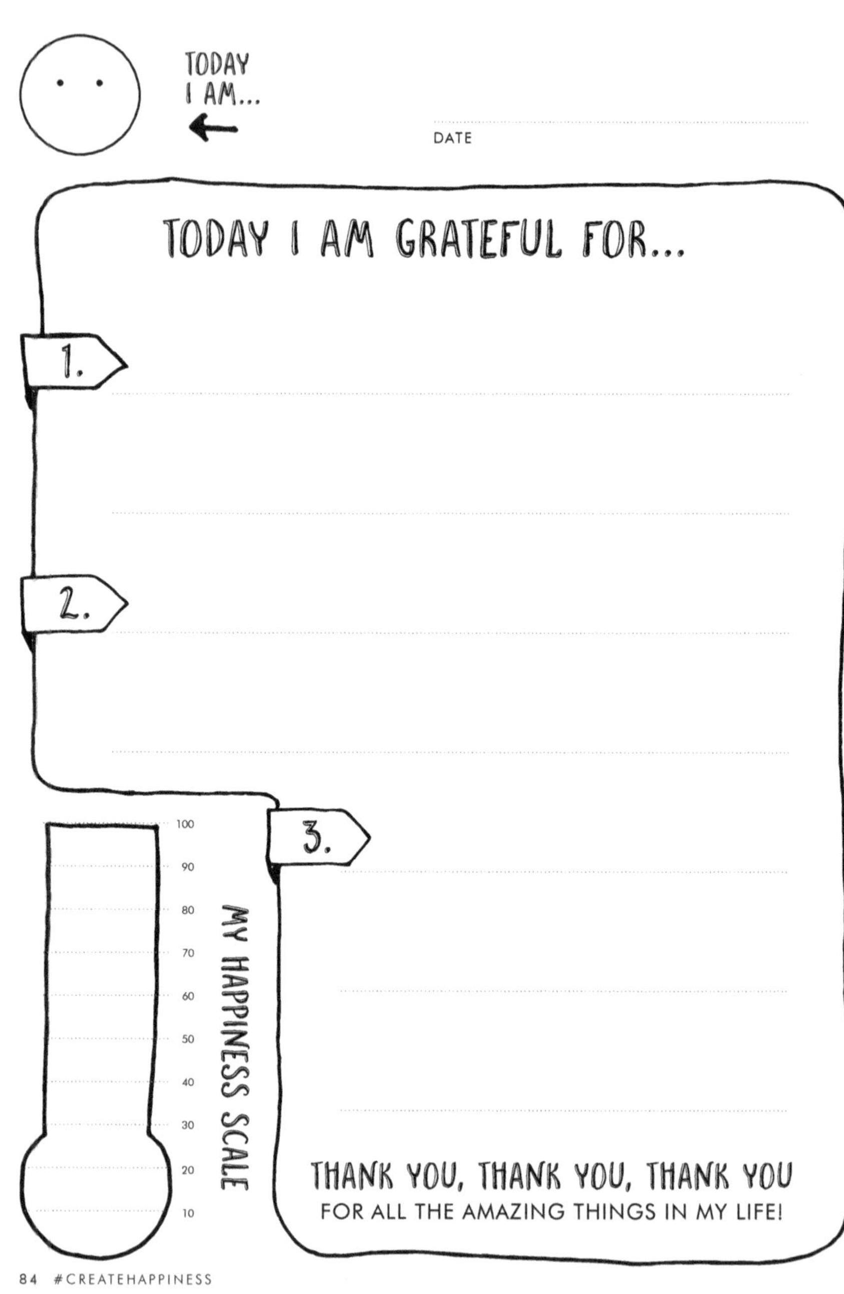
TODAY I AM...

DATE

TODAY I AM GRATEFUL FOR...

1.

2.

3.

100
90
80
70
60
50
40
30
20
10

MY HAPPINESS SCALE

THANK YOU, THANK YOU, THANK YOU
FOR ALL THE AMAZING THINGS IN MY LIFE!

TODAY I AM GRATEFUL FOR...

TODAY I AM... →

1.

2.

3.

THANK YOU, THANK YOU, THANK YOU
FOR ALL THE AMAZING THINGS IN MY LIFE!

MY HAPPINESS SCALE

100
90
80
70
60
50
40
30
20
10

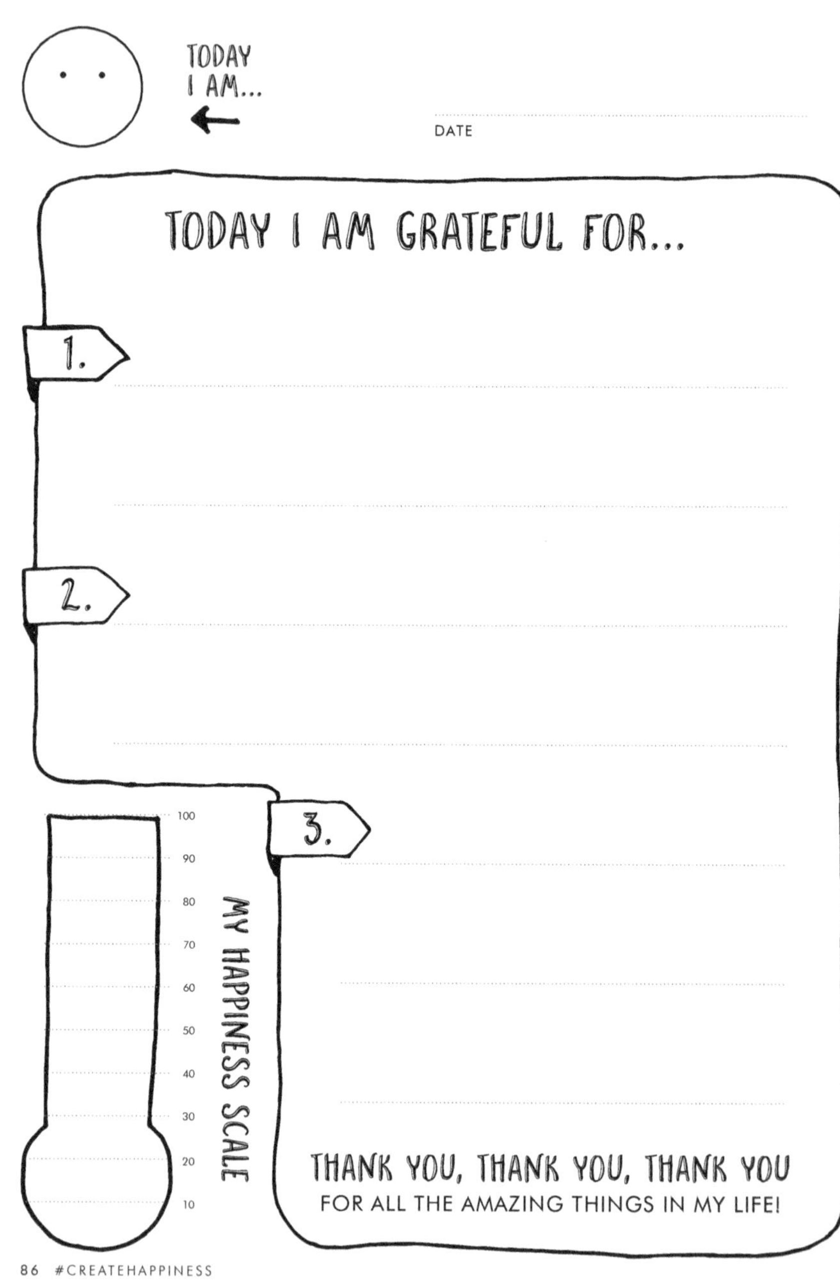

TODAY I AM...
DATE
TODAY I AM GRATEFUL FOR...
1.
2.
3.
100
90
80
70
60
50
40
30
20
10
MY HAPPINESS SCALE
THANK YOU, THANK YOU, THANK YOU
FOR ALL THE AMAZING THINGS IN MY LIFE!

TODAY I AM GRATEFUL FOR...

1.

2.

3.

THANK YOU, THANK YOU, THANK YOU
FOR ALL THE AMAZING THINGS IN MY LIFE!

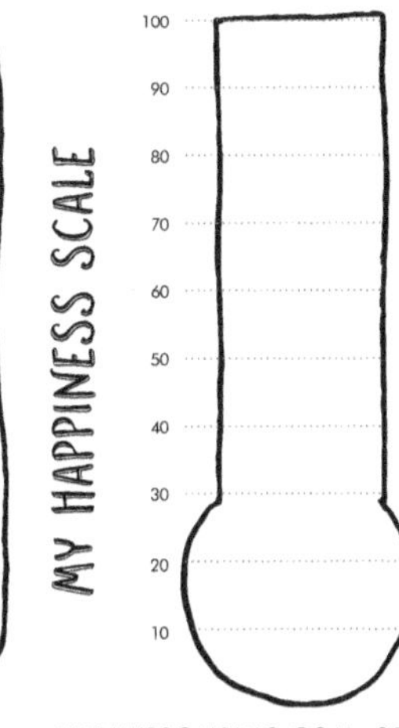

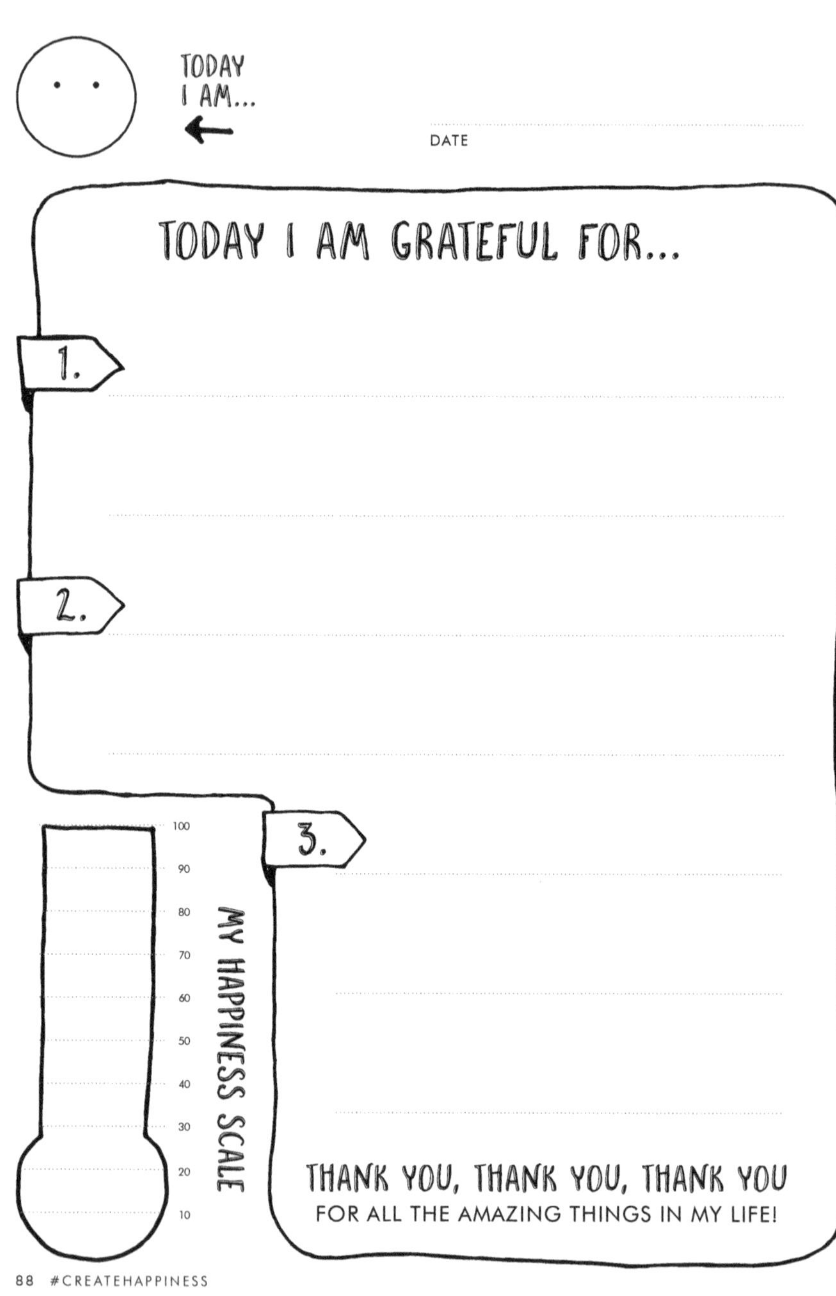

TODAY
I AM...
DATE
TODAY I AM GRATEFUL FOR...
1.
2.
3.
100
90
80
70
60
50
40
30
20
10
MY HAPPINESS SCALE
THANK YOU, THANK YOU, THANK YOU
FOR ALL THE AMAZING THINGS IN MY LIFE!

TODAY I AM GRATEFUL FOR...

1.

2.

3.

THANK YOU, THANK YOU, THANK YOU
FOR ALL THE AMAZING THINGS IN MY LIFE!

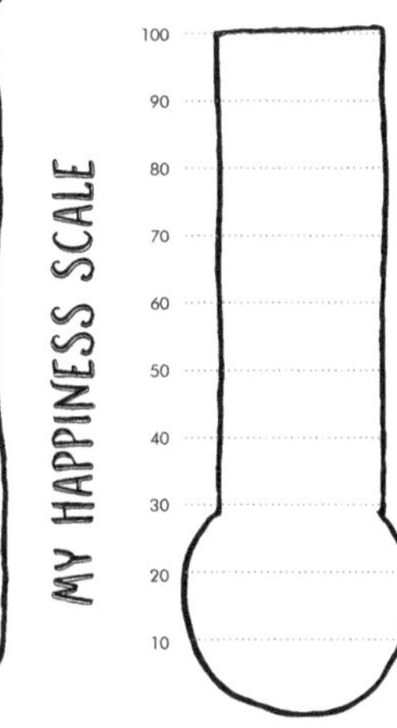

DO something NICE for SOMEONE ELSE

HAPPINESS TIP:

Giving to others releases natural feel-good chemicals in your brain that activate those areas (of the brain) associated with trust, pleasure and social connection. Spending money or doing something for others leads to higher levels of happiness, and increases the chance that you will be generous in the future. This creates a positive feedback loop of generosity and happiness. The trick is to do something without being asked.

THINGS I CAN DO
FOR SOMEONE ELSE

USE WORDS AND PICTURES TO SHOW YOUR IDEAS

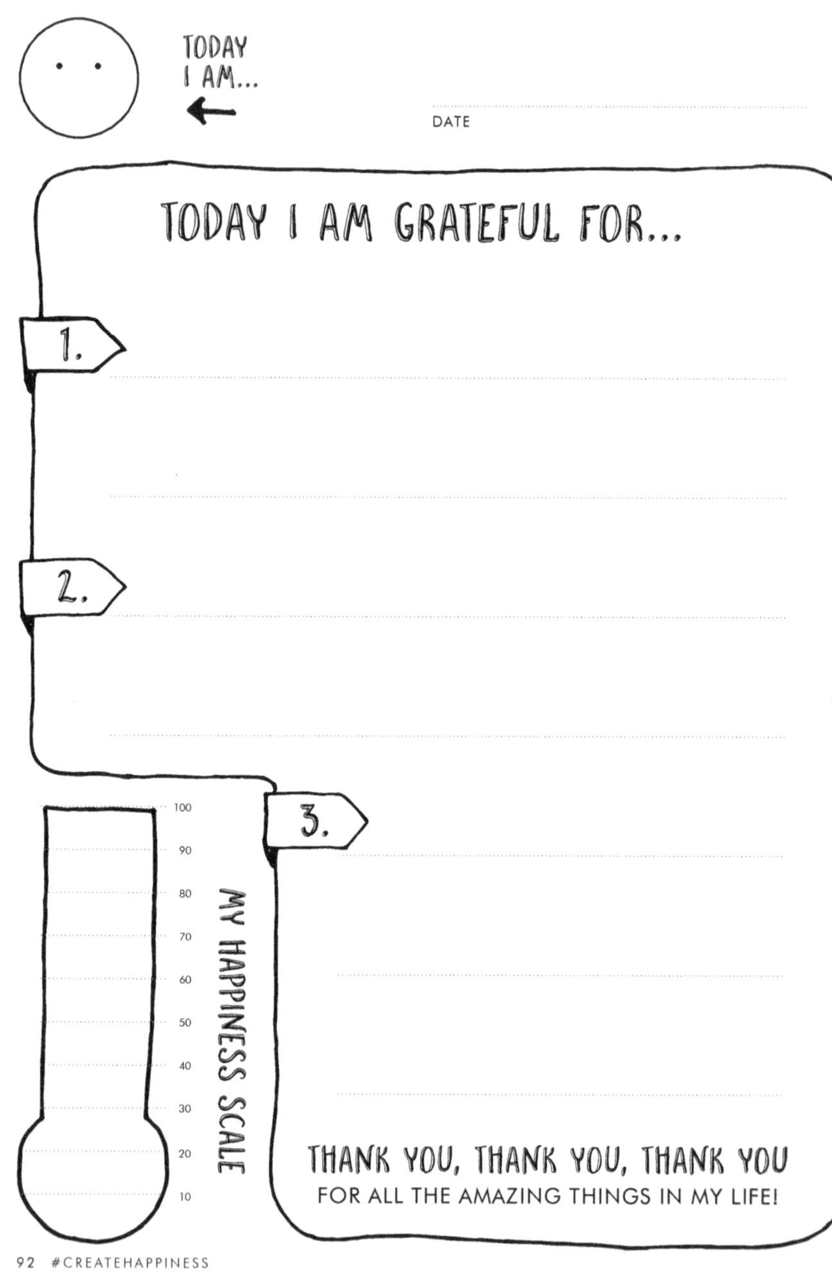

TODAY I AM...
DATE
TODAY I AM GRATEFUL FOR...
1.
2.
3.
MY HAPPINESS SCALE
100
90
80
70
60
50
40
30
20
10
THANK YOU, THANK YOU, THANK YOU
FOR ALL THE AMAZING THINGS IN MY LIFE!

TODAY
I AM...
→

TODAY I AM GRATEFUL FOR...

1.

2.

3.

THANK YOU, THANK YOU, THANK YOU
FOR ALL THE AMAZING THINGS IN MY LIFE!

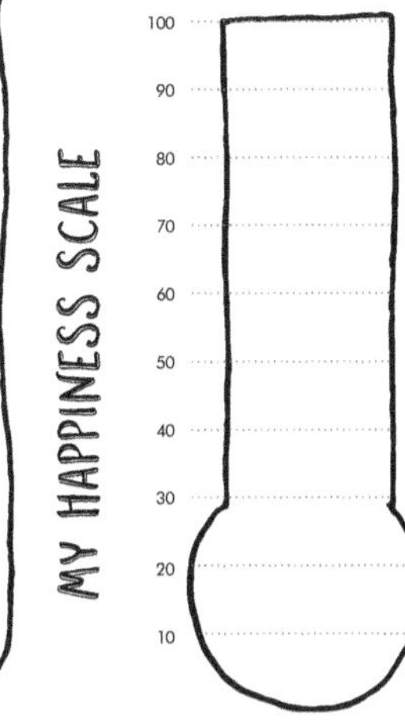

TODAY I AM...
DATE
TODAY I AM GRATEFUL FOR...
1.
2.
3.
MY HAPPINESS SCALE
100
90
80
70
60
50
40
30
20
10
THANK YOU, THANK YOU, THANK YOU
FOR ALL THE AMAZING THINGS IN MY LIFE!

TODAY I AM GRATEFUL FOR...

1.

2.

3.

THANK YOU, THANK YOU, THANK YOU
FOR ALL THE AMAZING THINGS IN MY LIFE!

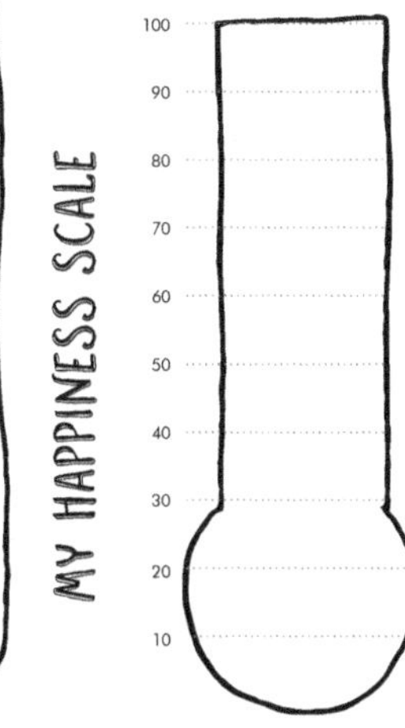

TODAY
I AM...

DATE

TODAY I AM GRATEFUL FOR...

1.

2.

3.

100
90
80
70
60
50
40
30
20
10

MY HAPPINESS SCALE

THANK YOU, THANK YOU, THANK YOU
FOR ALL THE AMAZING THINGS IN MY LIFE!

DATE

TODAY I AM GRATEFUL FOR...

1.

2.

3.

THANK YOU, THANK YOU, THANK YOU
FOR ALL THE AMAZING THINGS IN MY LIFE!

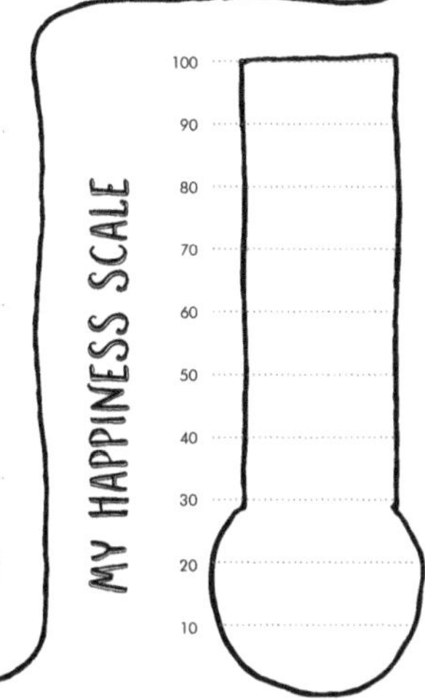

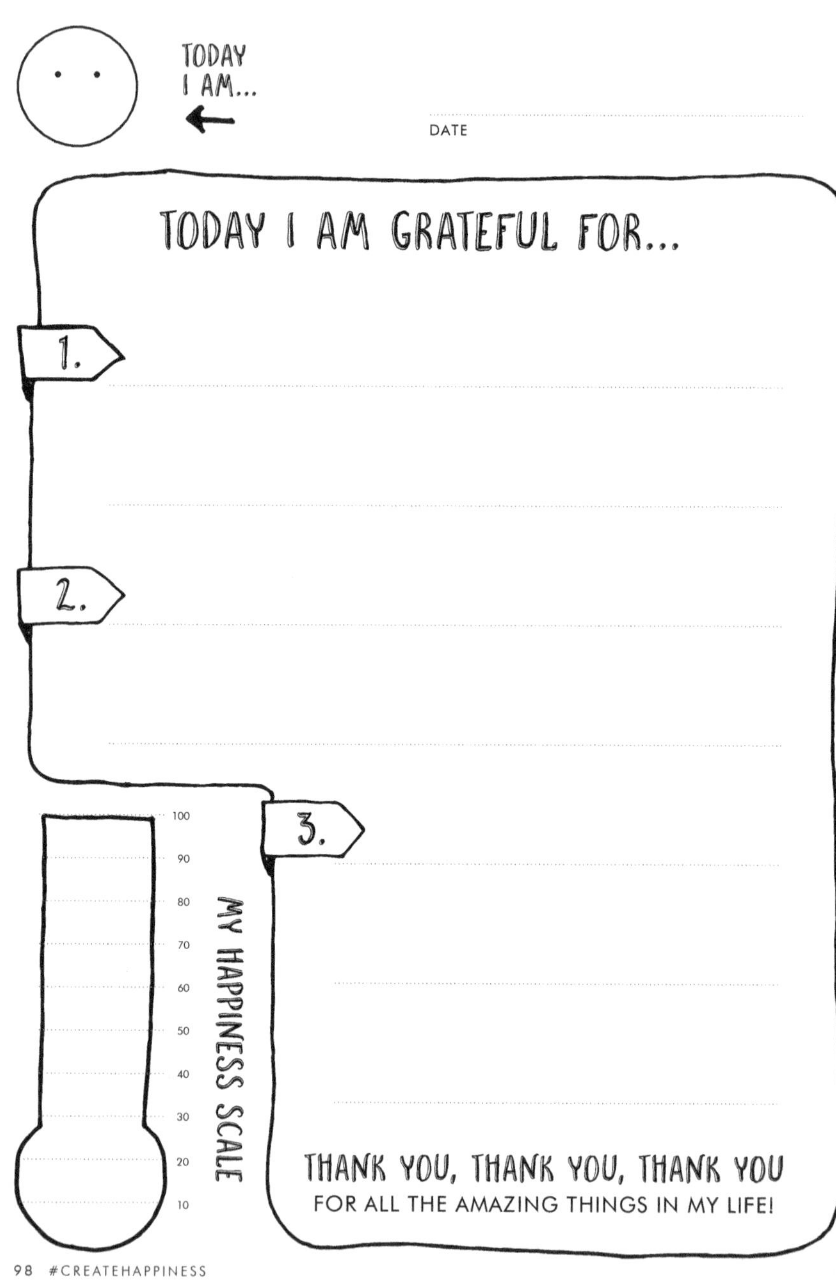

TODAY I AM...
DATE
TODAY I AM GRATEFUL FOR...
1.
2.
3.
MY HAPPINESS SCALE
100
90
80
70
60
50
40
30
20
10
THANK YOU, THANK YOU, THANK YOU
FOR ALL THE AMAZING THINGS IN MY LIFE!

....
DATE

TODAY I AM GRATEFUL FOR...

1.

2.

3.

THANK YOU, THANK YOU, THANK YOU
FOR ALL THE AMAZING THINGS IN MY LIFE!

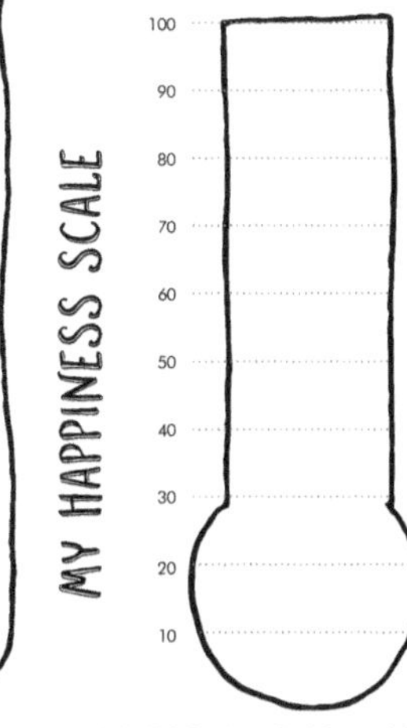

SAY ★ THANK ★ YOU

HAPPINESS TIP:

Say 'Thank you' as much as you can to as many people as you can. Thank them for the little things, like letting you in front of them in line, but also for the big stuff too, like your parents for caring for you or a teacher that believes in you.

Not only will it make them feel happy but it will make you feel more positive emotions, relish good experiences, improve your health, plus help you deal with difficult situations and build stronger relationships with others.

DRAWING BY LILY, AGE 9

TODAY
I AM...
DATE
TODAY I AM GRATEFUL FOR...
1.
2.
3.
100
90
80
70
60
50
40
30
20
10
MY HAPPINESS SCALE
THANK YOU, THANK YOU, THANK YOU
FOR ALL THE AMAZING THINGS IN MY LIFE!

DATE

TODAY I AM GRATEFUL FOR...

1.

2.

3.

THANK YOU, THANK YOU, THANK YOU
FOR ALL THE AMAZING THINGS IN MY LIFE!

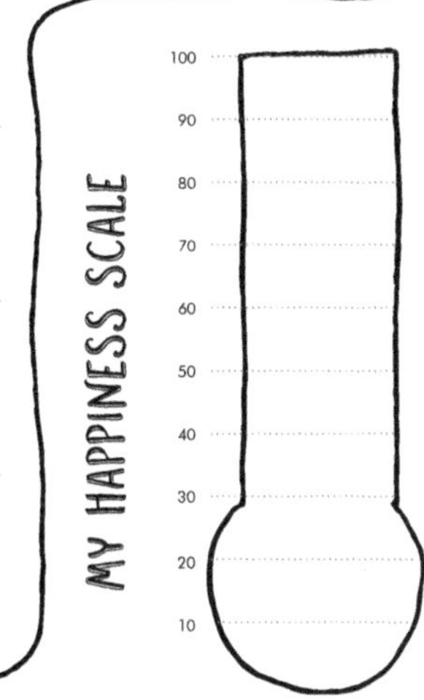

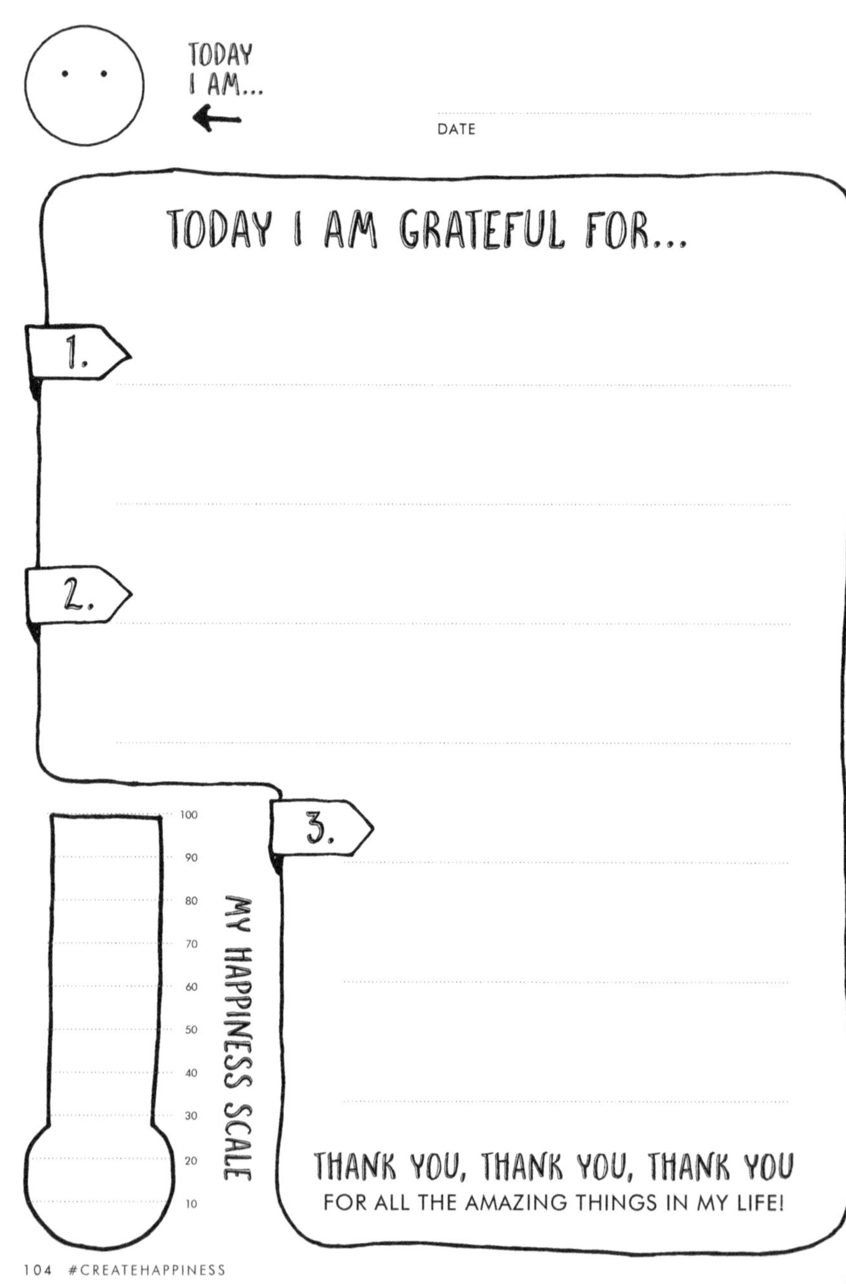

TODAY I AM...
DATE
TODAY I AM GRATEFUL FOR...
1.
2.
3.
MY HAPPINESS SCALE
100
90
80
70
60
50
40
30
20
10
THANK YOU, THANK YOU, THANK YOU
FOR ALL THE AMAZING THINGS IN MY LIFE!

....
DATE

TODAY I AM GRATEFUL FOR...

1.

2.

3.

THANK YOU, THANK YOU, THANK YOU
FOR ALL THE AMAZING THINGS IN MY LIFE!

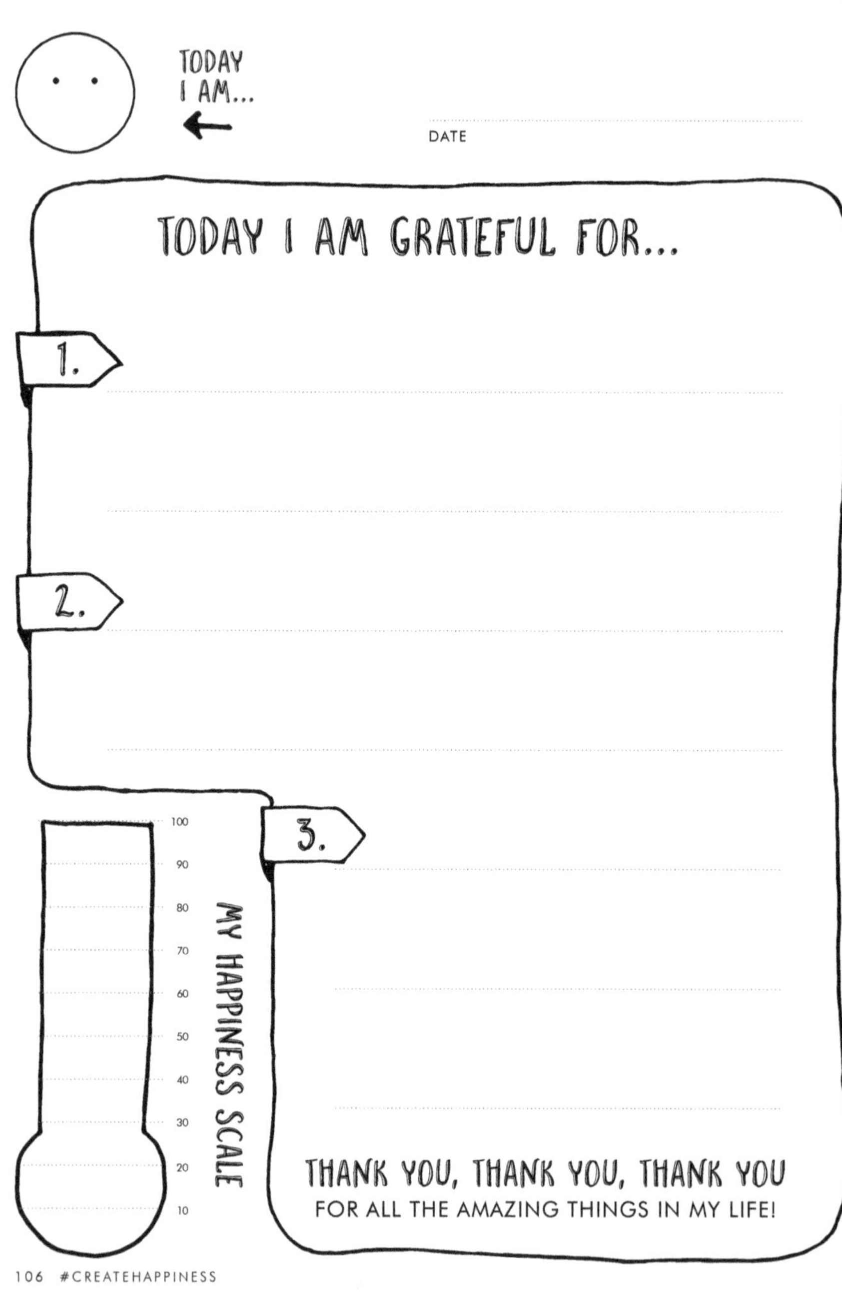

TODAY I AM...
DATE
TODAY I AM GRATEFUL FOR...
1.
2.
3.
100
90
80
70
60
50
40
30
20
10
MY HAPPINESS SCALE
THANK YOU, THANK YOU, THANK YOU
FOR ALL THE AMAZING THINGS IN MY LIFE!

....
DATE

TODAY I AM GRATEFUL FOR...

1.

2.

3.

THANK YOU, THANK YOU, THANK YOU
FOR ALL THE AMAZING THINGS IN MY LIFE!

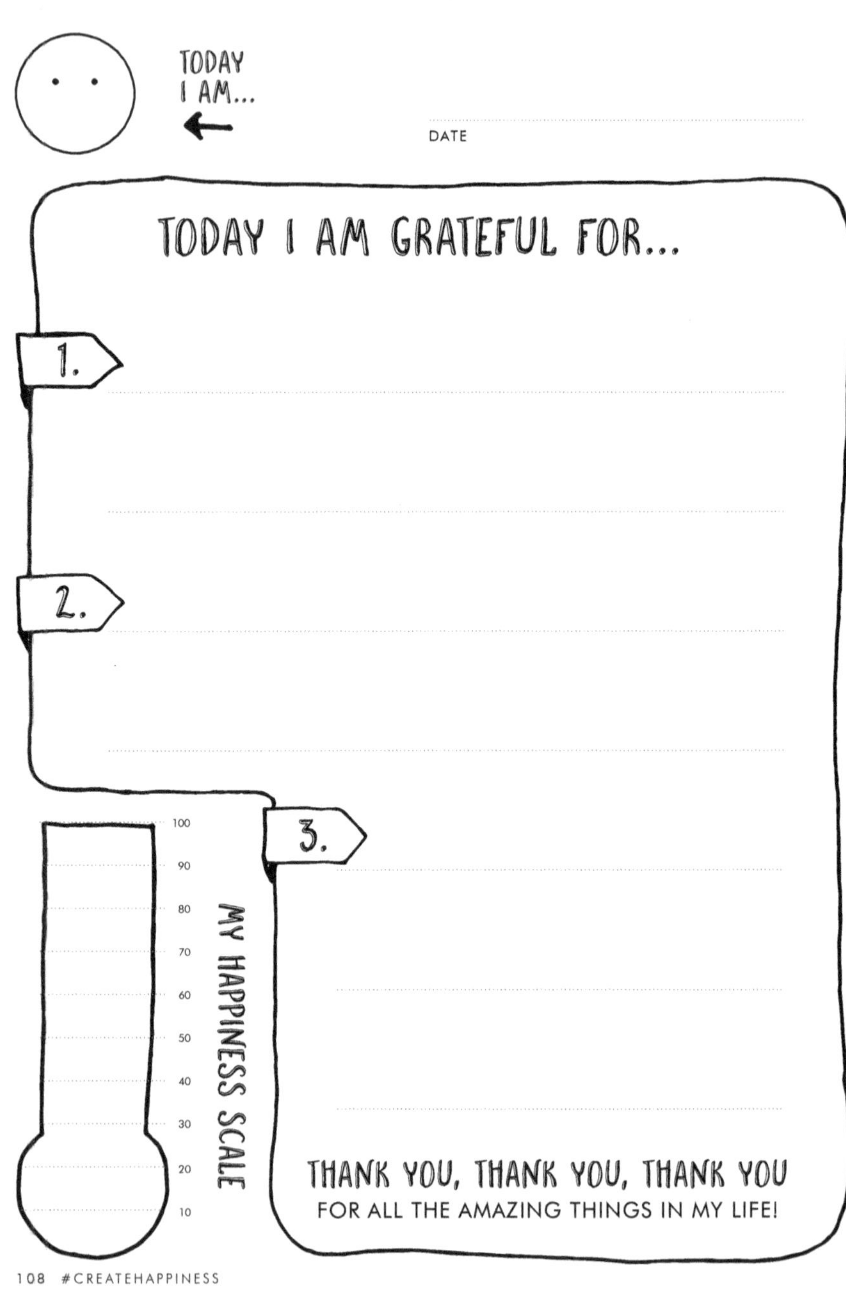

TODAY I AM...
DATE
TODAY I AM GRATEFUL FOR...
1.
2.
3.
MY HAPPINESS SCALE
100
90
80
70
60
50
40
30
20
10
THANK YOU, THANK YOU, THANK YOU
FOR ALL THE AMAZING THINGS IN MY LIFE!

DATE

TODAY I AM GRATEFUL FOR...

1.

2.

3.

THANK YOU, THANK YOU, THANK YOU
FOR ALL THE AMAZING THINGS IN MY LIFE!

MY HAPPINESS SCALE

100
90
80
70
60
50
40
30
20
10

Gratitude strengthens the immune system, lowers blood pressure, reduces symptoms of illness, and makes us less bothered by aches and pains. It also encourages us to exercise more and take better care of our health.[1]

7 WAYS GRATITUDE HELPS YOU

You can feel more connected to your friends, family, feel better about your school, have higher levels of optimism, increased life satisfaction, and decreased negative feelings.

It helps us notice the world around us, and what our blessings are. We start taking less things for granted and feel more awake and alive.[5]

Writing down 3 things you are grateful for can boost happiness better than recalling three times when a person felt a sense of pride in his or her own accomplishments...

It makes people look for the good in their life more, so it trains their attention to more good things.[7]

1. PROF. ROBERT EMMONS, THE UNIVERSITY OF CALIFORNIA & PROF. MICHAEL MCCULLOUGH, UNIVERSITY OF MIAMI
2. ACCORDING TO A STUDY PRESENTED AT AN AMERICAN PSYCHOLOGICAL ASSOCIATION CONVENTION
3. JEFFREY FROH, ASSOCIATE PROFESSOR, HOFSTRA UNIVERSITY
4. JEFFREY FROH, ASSOCIATE PROFESSOR, HOFSTRA UNIVERSITY
5. DR. KERRY HOWELLS, UNIVERSITY OF TASMANIA
6. DR. EMILIANA SIMON-THOMAS, SCIENCE DIRECTOR, THE GREATER GOOD SCIENCE CENTER, BERKELEY
7. PROF. PHILLIP WATKINS, DEPT OF PSYCHOLOGY, EASTERN WASHINGTON UNIVERSITY

For more facts go to *http://greatergood.berkeley.edu/topic/gratitude*

9 780473 425920